FAR HORIZONS

On the far edges of civilized space, brave and determined COLONISTS *behold the horizons of new worlds. Beyond the Empire's reach, they struggle to build new lives for themselves and their families.*

Together they must battle hostile creatures, vicious storms, and merciless pirate marauders. Failure will see the ruins of their homes buried by the sands of time. But if these settlers succeed, they can build brave new worlds on the Outer Rim....

CREDITS

LEAD DEVELOPER
Sam Stewart

WRITING AND ADDITIONAL DEVELOPMENT
Lisa Farrell, Sterling Hershey, Keith Ryan Kappel, and Jason Marker with Daniel Lovat Clark and Max Brooke

EDITING AND PROOFREADING
Mark Pollard and Paul Poppleton

MANAGING RPG PRODUCER
Chris Gerber

GAME LINE GRAPHIC DESIGN
EDGE Studio, David Ardila, and Chris Beck

EXPANSION GRAPHIC DESIGN
Chris Beck, Crystal Nichols, and Duane Nichols

GRAPHIC DESIGN MANAGER
Brian Schomburg

MANAGING ART DIRECTOR
Andrew Navaro

ART DIRECTION
Zoë Robinson and John M. Taillon

COVER ART
David Kegg and Mark Molnar

INTERIOR ART
Sara Betsy, Jon Bosco, Matt Bradbury, Christopher Burdett, Caravan Studio, JB Casacop, Mariusz Gandzel, David Griffith, Jeff Lee Johnson, Jason Juta, Adam Lane, Mark Molnar, Wibben, and the Lucasfilm art archives

PRODUCTION MANAGEMENT
Eric Knight

EXECUTIVE GAME DESIGNER
Corey Konieczka

EXECUTIVE PRODUCER
Michael Hurley

PUBLISHER
Christian T. Petersen

PLAYTESTERS
"Death Star Contractors" Doug Ruff with Craig Atkins, Mark Charlesworth, Julian Garner, Josh Jupp, and Nathan Wilkinson. "MadAdventurers Society" Tomas Hughes with Brian Casey, Rob Davee, and Jason Phillips. Michelle Ledbetter. "Morse's Marauders" Daniel Lovat Clark with Max Brooke, Andrew Fischer, Katrina Ostrander, and Sam Stewart.

LUCAS LICENSING

DIRECTOR OF PUBLISHING
Carol Roeder

SENIOR EDITOR
Jennifer Heddle

MANAGER OF THE HOLOCRON
Leland Chee

FANTASY FLIGHT GAMES

Fantasy Flight Games
1995 West County Road B2
Roseville, MN 55113
USA

ISBN 978-1-61661691-5   Product Code: SWE10

For more information about the *Star Wars*: EDGE OF THE EMPIRE line, free downloads, answers to rule queries, or just to pass on greetings, visit us online at

www.FantasyFlightGames.com

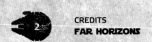

TABLE OF CONTENTS

t had been a long day already. The dead body just made it longer.

"I want that no-good ghhhk-oil salesman strung up for the murder of my boy!" Solk Horgon shouted.

I leaned against the doorframe of the marshal's office. "Solk, you may be king nerf baron 'round here, but we've got law and order in this town, same as any other."

"I didn't see no 'law and order' when they found my Seth behind the theater with his neck broke!" Horgon snarled. "Now you hang that Chevin, or step aside and let me."

I none too subtly tapped my hands on the holsters of my twin pistols. "Alchibi'll stand trial, and if he's guilty, he hangs. Not before. Now get on back to your ranch."

Horgon's face got even darker. "You haven't heard the last of this, Marshal!" He turned on his heels and stormed down the street.

I sighed and walked back inside my office. From the containment cell in the far corner, my prisoner watched me soberly.

"I appreciate you not 'stringing me up,' Marshal Sterne," Alchibi Des said in his booming, rumbling voice.

"Day's not over yet, Alchi." I plopped down at my desk, calling up the crime scene holos. Seth Horgon stared up blindly from the alley dirt, his neck snapped cleanly. "You still haven't given me an alibi for last night, and you're plenty strong enough to do the deed. Plus you and the Horgons haven't been on the best of terms."

"It is compelling, though circumstantial," Alchibi replied. "But I was in a confidential meeting."

"You stick with that story, you might as well tighten the noose yourself," I grumbled. "Listen, Alichi–"

"Hi Marshal! Hi Alchi!" A young, well-built Twi'lek popped in through the door.

I grunted. "What are you doing here, Mali?"

Malisan held up a basket of food. "Brought Alchi lunch from the ranch. Better than the reheated Imperial Army rations you eat, Marshal."

A Chevin's face wasn't built for smiling, but Alchibi brightened slightly. "Malisan. You are too kind. But you should be spending your break practicing your dance performance, not bringing me food. Besides, if Horgon catches one of his indentures bringing me lunch—"

"Oh, nonsense," Malisan sat the basket on my desk and started pulling roasted nerf and tubers out of it. After a moment, he looked up at me—and the crime holos. I saw the worry behind his cheerful demeanor.

"They're not going to hang him, are they?"

"Not if he's innocent, Mali," I replied, and wished I believed it.

"You're not going to hang him, Solk!" I shouted.

Horgon and his hired hands responded with a volley of blaster fire that lit up the night sky, blew in the rest of the windows, and set the door on fire.

"You missed!" I hollered, and sent a shot through the window into the darkened street. Malisan crouched in the corner of the office. He had returned to spend time with Alchibi; and, like me, was trapped when Horgon and his crew returned for some mob justice.

From his cell, Alchibi shook his head somberly. "Marshal Sterne. The situation seems dire. I would rather surrender than see you and Malisan dead."

I opened my mouth to tell him not to be an idiot, but Mali beat me to it. "No, you can't!" He stared at me, fear and guilt running across his face. "Marshal, you can't let him do that."

I looked at Mali for a long moment, then groaned. "Ah, hell. Alchi, you were meeting with Mali at the theater last night, weren't you?"

Mali looked guilty, but also relieved. "He was going to buy out my indenture contract from Horgon. Sponsor my dancing. But he didn't kill Seth."

"No," I shook my head. "I'm guessing you did that."

Mali looked sick. "Seth told Alchi he wouldn't sell my contract. He said I'd be stuck herding nerfs all my life. He said he liked seeing an indenture 'in his proper place.' He, he laughed. I just...snapped. I didn't mean to hurt him."

The three of us sat there, looking at each other for a long moment. Then another blaster bolt punched through the wall. "Send him out, Sterne," Horgon bellowed. "Or we'll burn you out!"

"Oh, to hell with it." I scrambled across the floor, hitting the containment cell's control panel. The energy barrier flickered out as I kicked my desk away from the trap door hidden beneath it. Alchibi and Malisan stared at me.

"Well, what are you two waiting for?" I snarled. "It leads out of town." I punched in the combination to the office safe, and pulled out the thermal detonator I'd confiscated from the spice runners three months ago. "I just need to cover our tracks."

A half hour later, we stood on the hill outside town and watched the townsfolk putting out the last of the fire that consumed my office. That was good; I really hadn't wanted to burn down all of Main Street.

Alchibi snuffled. "I am sorry about this, Marshal." Malisan nodded silently.

"Oh, Horgon was a jerk anyway, and his son was no good trash," I grinned wryly. "On the other hand, looks like I'm out a job. If you're still going off-planet, can I tag along?"

COLONIZING THE EDGE

Colonists are the galaxy's movers and shakers, from true world-builders in the wilds of outer space to social masters that use their influence and personal charisma to advance their own agendas. FAR HORIZONS expands on the Colonist career presented in the EDGE OF THE EMPIRE Core Rulebook, offering new ideas and details for existing specializations while expanding the career with three new specializations. Whether struggling against krayt dragons and Tusken Raiders on the windswept dunes of Tatooine or running a space station on the darkest edges of Wild Space, players using this book will find something useful for everyone.

Chapter I: Building Better Worlds focuses on the Colonist career itself. It discusses and adds new Colonist-specific backgrounds, Motivations, and Obligations. It introduces the Arcona, Chevin, and Gran—three new playable species that are especially well suited to

be Colonists. It also adds three new specializations— the Entrepreneur, Marshal, and Performer—along with their requisite talent trees. All Colonist specializations gain the benefit of two new Signature Abilities, boosting Colonists who use them to an elite status.

Chapter II: Law and Ordnance introduces new weapons, a substantial amount of new gear, and a selection of new vehicles preferred by Colonists.

Chapter III: New Horizons Await provides advice for creating Colonist-based adventures, ideas concerning how to integrate Colonists in the story, and ways to build and highlight social encounters. The chapter includes advice for GM and player collaboration on Colonist storylines. Chapter III also covers Colonist campaigns, rewards, and advice for Game Masters wishing to successfully integrate Colonist characters into a story.

COLONISTS IN THE GALAXY

For millennia, colonists have provided spacefaring societies with the manpower and drive to expand across the galaxy. The ever-growing Republic, Empire, and other civilizations create a perpetual need for resources, living space, and political separation, so colonization of new worlds continues to this day. While some periods of galactic history have witnessed a sharp decrease in colonization, there have always been beings with reasons to stake their claims on new worlds.

Although anyone can become a colonist, the best are typically smart, ambitious, tough, and willing to brave the unknown. They represent many fields of study or expertise, and often prefer non-combat roles. Colonist leaders are typically highly charismatic. Moreover, isolation from the galaxy at large drives a need for Colonists to be intelligent, leading most to focus on their own area of expertise, such as leadership, healing, and legitimate commerce. Some seek more personal goals, such as achieving celebrity. Others strive to bring order and civil protection to far-flung settlements.

TRUE COLONISTS

The ancient Republic's expansion outward from the Core Worlds relied on massive colonization efforts. While many early missions grew out of land and population constraints, later efforts were corporate driven, often the product of a land rush to claim new resources. The first galactic-scale colonization effort grew from

the Core Worlds into the Colonies region, many thousands of years ago. The Colonies became an extension of Core World attitudes, power, and ambition. These were true colonies—permanent settlements intended to expand the reach and resources of the homeworld. Eventually, distance and politics would divide many colonies from their home governments.

As colonization efforts developed, other worlds became little more than chunks of resources ripe for exploitation. This was especially true in the Expansion Region, where corporations raced to grab prime star systems before the region became officially open to Republic colonization efforts. These colonists were less adventurous explorers and settlers, and more entrepreneurial or exploited workers drawn to company-held planets where they found it difficult to leave.

In current times, colonization attempts usually delve beyond the fringes of Known Space. These missions attempt to push back the boundaries of Wild Space by either filling in poorly explored areas within Known Space or expanding at the fringes of the Outer Rim. Few attempts to colonize the Unknown Regions succeed. The hyperspace tangle at the borders of the Unknown Regions makes even successful colonies isolated and difficult to reach. However, even in these times, only a fraction of the stars in the galaxy have been visited and explored. A new colony can happen in any place, at any time.

THE ALLURE OF A NEW WORLD

It is often difficult for the non-colonist to understand the desire to establish a settlement on a new world in remote areas and under dangerous conditions. With tens of thousands of civilized planets to choose from, what exactly is the draw for forging ahead with yet another settlement on what is likely to be an unremarkable or inhospitable world? The reality is that age-old reasons still apply—breaking with current society or government, seeking to establish a civilization based on specific ideals, and exploiting resources.

With the rise of the Galactic Empire, more and more colonists have sought to escape the authoritarian practices of Emperor Palpatine. Enslaved species have fled to worlds beyond the boundaries of the Empire, trying to escape while they still can. Followers of the Force—those few remaining individuals who follow the Jedi Order or other, lesser known traditions—have escaped Vader's attempts to purge them from the galaxy. No matter the reason, most of these types of colonies seek isolation and secrecy to avoid Imperial pursuit. They may number anywhere from a few dozen Force users to several hundred or thousand species fleeing enslavement. Even the Rebel Alliance establishes the occasional secret colony in the form of safe worlds, hiding friends, families, and facilities far from Imperial reach.

A LITTLE CIVILIZATION

What separates a colony from the wild frontier is more than simply the presence of the colonists themselves, it is what the colonists bring with them: civilization. The most successful colonies have a system of governance, law and order, and at least a semblance of a functioning economy. After a few generations, some colonies become indistinguishable from the Core Worlds from which they sprang.

Civilization doesn't happen by accident. It's hard work, and requires coordination on the part of the colonists—in fact, it arguably consists exclusively of coordination between the colonists. Some colonists set out to recreate the society of their homeworld, importing the traditions and systems of government wholesale to their new planet. These colonists have at least the advantage of a template from which to work, and many successful colonies have flourished along these lines. Others, however, resolve to build a more perfect society than the one they left behind. These optimists tend to gather into ideological groups before they set out into the frontier, and it's an unfortunate truth that colonies founded for such ideological reasons are often done so in the least hospitable conditions and with inadequate supplies and support. Ideological colonists often wish to leave their homeworld because they are an oppressed or ignored underclass, and that status brings with it certain economic hardships that make establishing a colony even more dif-

Colonization of a new world naturally necessitates some exploration. However, there are many critical differences between the colonist and the explorer. The most obvious is that the colonist arrives on a new world expecting to make it his permanent home. The explorer, on the other hand, is more interested in discovering new places or civilizations, reporting them back to the galaxy at large or to his employer, and then moving to the next system.

Though the circumstances vary, a colonist typically arrives at a predetermined colonization site. While a few colony ships are sent blindly into deep space to find their own path and destination, it is far more common that they aim for a specific, well studied target. Though no world is completely known before colonists make it a permanent home, the planet in question is usually vetted and assessed for livability, cosmic hazards, health threats, native populations, and the harshness of the environment.

Colonists typically do not have the same level of wanderlust that drives dedicated explorers. Colonists are usually out to improve their own lives and that of their families, as determined by their personal desires and causes. Many explorers actually prefer the isolation of deep space and the freedom of movement without government, familial, or social interference.

ficult than it would be otherwise. Some Core Worlds societies are happy to get rid of their malcontents by sending them to a colony world, but for every enlightened schism on good terms there is an unscrupulous explorer, bureaucrat, or corporation happy to exploit the desires of ideological colonists for a quick credit.

However, not all colonial civilizations are the result of planning. In some cases, the transition from wild frontier to colony happens organically and the resulting civilization is improvised and often extremely heterogeneous. In these cases, the nature of the resulting civilization is shaped by the men and women who find themselves in the position to create it. A single charismatic town leader or a justice-loving marshal can transform the lawless frontier into a true colony by bringing a little civilization.

THE LIGHT OF KNOWLEDGE

The fruits of civilization are many, but arguably its most important benefit is education and learning. Scholars may also claim, biased as they are, that it is education that supports civilization, rather than the other way around.

In any case, colonies can benefit greatly from a few learned individuals. Doctors, teachers, and skilled technicians are always in short supply outside of the Core Worlds, and their presence or absence in a colony can make a profound difference to that colony's health and quality of life. Some accomplished specialists take on a semi-nomadic existence, traveling from colony to colony to spread the benefits of their expertise as widely as possible. Others find communities springing up wherever they choose to settle, as local colonists are more successful with access to the specialist's expertise.

Given the high demand, there's also a certain freedom to colony life for specialists. A struggling colony cannot afford to turn away a doctor who may not have exactly finished medical school, or one whose medical license may have been revoked by the ethics board of his homeworld. Capabilities matter more than credentials in the colonies, and an expert sawbones, scholar, or spanner-monkey can shine free of the stifling bureaucracy and requirements of the Core Worlds.

BUILDING A LIFE, BUILDING A NAME

Life on the edge of the galaxy is more free than life in the Core, and it's easier to get a start in a wide variety of trades or lifestyles. Colonies can't afford to turn away skilled help, and there's also less competition crowding out those who might not make the cut in the Core Worlds.

For some would-be business owners, performers, or tradespeople, the colonies represent a chance to make a name for themselves. A musical act that couldn't find booking on Coruscant might be the only show in town in a remote colony, and for some people being a big mynock in a small cave is preferable to total anonymity. Others treat the colonies as a stepping stone, using the opportunities there to get the experience and the credibility to bring their skills closer and closer to the Core Worlds.

Of course, the small-town feel of the edge can cut both ways. One bad performance or bungled job can haunt a colonist for years as word of mouth spreads. The unlimited potential of the frontier doesn't always translate to success. A chance is just a chance, after all.

A COLONIST'S LIFE

Other careers may be better suited to keeping the peace, but the Colonist is best suited to enjoying it. Some Colonists may be a part of a small community, helping to lead it toward growth and prosperity. Others might be more interested in escaping civilization altogether. These brave Colonists stay far afield of the nearest settlements, living off the land and going into town only a few times per year. However, the majority of new arrivals to a colony buy or build a shop tied to their trade and as close to a popular cantina as possible. Other Colonists may perform house calls, or work out of their homes or a local trading post.

Despite their best intentions, not all Colonists live out their lives on their adopted homeworld. Some become swept up in events and find themselves caught in interplanetary adventures. On other backwater worlds, the Colonist is able to quickly adapt and fit in, presuming the climate and culture aren't too different from what he is accustomed to. Most colonies share enough similarities that Colonists can make themselves at home quickly. However, on ecumenopolis worlds like Denon or Coruscant, or extreme environments that are complete opposites of their home colonies, the Colonist tends to come off as a wide-eyed tourist at best, and an easy target or ignorant hayseed at worst. Fortunately, earnest farm-boy innocence goes a long way to charm even the most cynical city-dweller, and most trespasses are forgiven.

BUILDING BETTER WORLDS

"Our operation is small enough not to be noticed—which is advantageous for everyone."

–Baron-Administrator Lando Calrissian

The galaxy is a big place, and getting bigger all the time. Every time a habitable planet is discovered, some intrepid souls volunteer to leave behind everything they know in favor of the new world. These brave individuals are called Colonists. The Colonist is generally educated or skilled in a particular trade and travels to a sparsely populated world on the fringe of the galaxy to start over. Some Colonists are motivated by greed, others want to forge a legacy on the new world, and some seek an escape from their meaningless lives. Many settlers have only ever lived on the frontier, born generations after the original colony ship landed. Some of these restless souls look toward the Core with dreams of escaping their rustic backwater world, never truly understanding what made their ancestors flee in the first place.

The galaxy turns on the prevalence of Colonists, as they make up much of the galaxy's labor force. Colonists are the cogs that keep the galaxy spinning, and they account for an overwhelming majority of the galactic economy. In the private sector, these individuals represent most business owners, from local shops

to galactic-scale corporations. They may also work for these businesses as clerks, researchers, bookkeepers and accountants, public relations personnel, and even private security. Colonists also include most beings in arts or entertainment, food production, raw material collection, and healthcare. In addition to making up the bulk of the private sector, Colonists account for many government employees, including administrators, executives, lawyers, educators, and even some members of the military and law enforcement.

Generally speaking, most pioneers were born somewhere in the Core Worlds, and for various reasons—often economic or political—they chose to leave everything behind and travel to the Outer Rim to start a new life. These beings can be anyone, from the most destitute and homeless who leave in search of work, to retiring politicians or election night losers looking to start fresh or field test new ideas in government. In between, there are physicians unable to procure residencies and researchers seeking to study frontier life or new species of flora and fauna. There are law enforcement officers weary of high-risk spice busts who want to retire to a life of tracking down shaak tippers, and artists looking for inspiration by the unspoiled, grand vistas of an untamed world. There are criminals under new aliases, trying to escape their crimes and start over, and there are respectable businesspeople, launching new ventures far away from the corporate-dominated markets of the Core.

Still, no matter what plans someone might make on his way to a colony, everything changes dirtside.

Someone who sought life as a humble farmer could find himself elected mayor. A former biology student might be forced to replace the colony doctor, or asked to use his expertise to feed the entire community. When populations are small, social pressure can be intense for those even marginally qualified to perform skilled work. Everyone has a responsibility to the well-being of all, or else the colony isn't likely to survive long after initial supplies run dry.

A GALAXY TO SETTLE

Chapter I: Building Better Worlds presents a wealth of options and advice for players and GMs regarding the creation and advancement of Colonist characters. This chapter offers expanded backgrounds, Obligations, and Motivations for Colonist characters.

Chapter I also offers three new species to players at character creation. The Gran, Chevin, and Arcona are naturally suited to the socially focused work of Colonists, but can succeed in any career. The notoriously social and communal Gran have established a number of successful colonies on worlds like Hok and Malastare, not to mention their contributions to countless others. The selfless "we" mentality of Arconan society has given them a reputation as easily duped rubes when off Cona, but their willingness to work toward what is best for the group makes them valued additions to any colony ship. The Chevin have an earned reputation as slavers across the galaxy, a practice not all Chevin off Vinsoth approve of or participate in. However, Chevin are hard-nosed, competitive traders, no matter what commodity they might trade. While these three species are all associated with peaceful and

professional lifestyles, there are always exceptions. In any case, these species are excellent choices for players creating a Colonist character.

The chapter also contains three new Colonist specializations. The Entrepreneur is a credits-obsessed character with a nose for opportunity. The Marshal can track a suspect through every cantina and bolt-hole on the planet, and is a quick hand with a blaster. Performers are used to having their way, and can charm or distract the opposition equally well.

Additionally, two Colonist signature ability trees add powerful new abilities for any Colonist character. Each advance taken on the tree improves the effectiveness of the already-powerful signature ability. For a knowledgeable professional, Insightful Revelation allows a Player Character to learn or realize a valuable piece of information that would have otherwise gone unnoticed at a critical time. Some call it adrenaline, or being in the "zone" or a "flow-state." Others liken it to divine intervention. Meanwhile, Unmatched Expertise allows a Player Character to function as a master of his chosen field, putting on a skillful display of his trade long enough to overcome challenges that would normally be beyond the party.

COLONIST BACKGROUNDS

Colonists can come from almost any walk of life, as there are as many reasons a colonist might decide to move to a new world as there are colonies in the known galaxy. Anything from the lure of open spaces and fresh air to desiring to escape the Empire or the law can drive a Colonist to volunteer for a one-way trip to the Outer Rim, Wild Space, or even the Unknown Regions. Still, what a Colonist's life was before boarding the colony ship and what it becomes when he makes planetfall can often be two very different things. It is important to take all of this into consideration to create a Colonist character who is multifaceted and interesting.

The romanticized image of the Colonist might be that of Core World aristocrats and tradespeople unloading supplies from a colony ship, but not every Colonist books passage on the very first ship to a new world. Many join more established colonies, some settled centuries or even millennia before. Even long-standing, successful colonies are usually in need of skilled professionals in the fields of medicine and education. Freighter pilots usually pass the word along the hyperlanes, though colonies sometimes hunt skilled individuals through professional recruiting services. Qualified professionals answering the call of those in need often arrive to a grateful town willing to provide a home, a place of business, and an almost endless supply of hot meals and courtship opportunities.

While the backgrounds for some Colonist characters might detail their lives just before boarding a colony ship, many colonist families have lived several generations without ever leaving the colonized world. Tatooine has been settled multiple times over thousands of years, but because life on the desert world is so difficult, the population has struggled to grow beyond a loose collection of settlements. Of the thousand-thousand worlds, many still fit this description. Those born on these perpetual backwaters still live the hardscrabble life of the Colonist, and while that life can be tough and unforgiving, they seek to make life just a little bit easier for the next generation.

During character creation, players should spend some time thinking about how their characters got to the starting point in their campaigns. Everyone comes from somewhere, and a being that ends up living on a rustic backwater when he was born in a Core World commercial high rise might well have an origin story more captivating than most. The following are various concepts for the background history of a Colonist in Edge of the Empire. These are meant to be starting points for character creation, and only represent a small facet of who a character is and what matters to him. In order to create layered, three-dimensional characters, players may seek to shape their choices in skills, equipment, and Obligations based upon a background narrative such as those provided here.

THE OPPORTUNIST

Founding a colony is hard work, but a generation or two later, when the hardest work is done but opportunity still abounds, the opportunist moves in with fresh resources. These characters are often looked down upon by already established families, especially those opportunists seeking a leadership position before the landing ramp is even fully extended. There are also colonies with corporate or Imperial interests, where a bureaucrat offworld might send in new leadership that has minimal experience. Opportunists are, at their core, enthusiastic and willing to take any risk, but often lack a key understanding of the beings they intend to influence. In truth, this understanding can only come with time.

Doctors may be some of the most welcome opportunists since their skills are so vital to a colony's success. A doctor might be a naive youngster moving out to a colony to make his fortune and gain vital experience before returning to the Core, or an older physician with a modest skill set who figures he might be able to make more money in a place where demand for doctors outweighs supply. In either case, their callow attitude or eccentricities may be tolerated by their new neighbors, who are just happy to have a doctor join the settlement.

On the other hand, **Entrepreneurs** are seldom welcome in a colony. Many Entrepreneurs see some aspect of a colony's success—a profitable mine, a good location for trade, or a local product that could generate off-world demand—as their chance to get rich quickly. Since Entrepreneurs work in the world of finance, investments, and asset acquisition, most locals have a hard time following what they do and distrust them as a result. That many Entrepreneurs don't have the locals' best interests at heart doesn't help the situation.

Performers generally earn a cautious welcome from the colonies they visit. The Performer gives the locals an entertaining evening to brighten their drab lives. However, a Performer can easily outstay his welcome. The locals tend to see Performers the same way that they see boisterous relatives: fun for a few days, but increasingly tiresome during long visits.

A **Politico** may be sent to a new colony as a representative of a larger political or commercial interest. Many colonies are founded by established governments or corporations, and those governments and corporations tend to want to ensure the colony stays loyal and profitable. Thus, they often pack the colonial administration with their own appointees. These appointees may be receiving the task as a reward for loyalty or previous services rendered, or as the next step in a promising career. Generally, however, they are chosen from outside the colony they will be running. Most colonists react to these off-world administrators with suspicion and resentment, seeing them as outside overlords sent to keep them in line.

Marshals who end up as opportunists may be in a similar position to that of the Politico. A Marshal who arrives in a colony may be sent by a larger law enforcement agency to bring law and order to a wild frontier. In that case, the locals are likely to respond with mistrust and resentment. However, sometimes a Marshal is brought in by some local community members who want to hire a professional to keep the peace in their settlement. In this case, the Marshal can at least count on the backing of some prominent individuals, but may also feel beholden to them.

Scholars may become opportunists when they travel to a settlement as part of their research. They may be studying some local phenomenon, or even studying the colony itself. In any case, their reception may depend entirely on their demeanor. A polite or deferential Scholar may earn the amused tolerance or even respect of the locals, while an arrogant or superior Scholar probably breeds resentment and hostility.

THE GRIZZLED SETTLER

This character usually began as a young idealist, perhaps newly married. He decided the best opportunities for his family were in starting over somewhere new, where the sweat off his back could build something lasting. Unfortunately, life on the frontier is hard, and what starts as a dream for the future can quickly turn sour as children succumb to exotic diseases or local wildlife, leaving some settlers stranded with nothing to live for. The grizzled settler has lived through the worst the planet has to offer, and if asked, takes a pessimistic view of any enterprise—if he does more than spit in response.

A **Politico** may have started out as a young and idealistic leader of a colony. In the past, he honestly believed he could build a new utopia in this new world, free from the corruption and graft of established planets. Eventually, however, he saw his world succumb to the same problems he thought he left behind, leaving him with an embittered view of his situation.

Years of watching patients succumb to local illness, accidents, and even violence could leave a **Doctor** with a grizzled and bitter outlook. He could be especially frustrated because he knows many of his patients would have survived had he possessed better tools and medicines than could be found on a backwater colony.

Likewise, a **Marshal** may have spent his entire career fighting against lawlessness and banditry, only to eventually realize that his fellow citizens didn't appreciate his efforts. Perhaps he watched his town descend into violence over some sort of feud, or the colony lynched one of his prisoners before the prisoner could be put on trial. In any case, this left the Marshal with a pessimistic view of his fellows, and the depressing realization that his life's work may have been in vain.

Entrepreneurs may have become colonists hoping to establish thriving businesses (or even full corporations) "from the ground up" in a new colony. They spent countless credits on their enterprise, only to see it fail due to disasters and ruinous cost overruns beyond their control. Now they're left with nothing, stranded in a colony they've come to loathe.

For every entertainer who makes it big, there are thousands who can barely scrape by in the galaxy. A **Performer** could have ended up

an unwilling colonist as he traveled from one poorly paying gig to another. Finally he settled down as the permanent entertainment of a local cantina. Now he spends his nights performing for the same, unappreciative crowd while knowing in his heart that he could have been a star given half a chance.

A **Scholar** may be a colonist with a deep love of learning and knowledge. However, given his finances and resources, a proper education and career in academia was always out of reach. Thus he became a self-taught researcher or historian, but without the credentials that establish him as a "proper" Scholar in the eyes of the larger galaxy.

THE FUGITIVE

The galaxy is full of those on the run from something or someone. Some people may be pursued by bounty hunters, while others may be fleeing local governments, corporations, or even the Empire. Many of these people are guilty of their accused crimes, while others are innocent victims of a miscarriage of justice. In either case, colonies provide a safe haven where a person can hide, reinvent themselves, and start over in life.

An **Entrepreneur** may be a fugitive after engineering a major scam or fraud in some of the large galactic markets. He could have made millions of credits before the authorities discovered his crimes. His accounts frozen, his assets stripped, he fled to the furthest colony he could find before he could be arrested.

A **Politico** or a **Performer** could be a dissident. Perhaps they stood up for what they believed in, and that put them in opposition to the Empire. They may have used their status as a known public persona to spread a message of defiance. Now they're on the run, marked for arrest (or even execution) by the Imperial authorities. Since they may have been a prominent figure in their previous life, their defiance is even more galling to the Empire.

A **Scholar** could have been a respected researcher for a corporation, until he made a terrible discovery in the course of his work. He realized that his invention or research could cause terrible harm, and he doubted his employer could resist the temptation of using it. His only recourse was to flee, vanishing from galactic society as best he could. In this case, the corporation doesn't just want the Scholar, they want the highly valuable knowledge he possesses.

Sadly, not all **Doctors** are motivated by idealism and the desire to help others. Some are disturbed, quacks, or even amateur researchers who view their patients as little more than the subjects of their "experiments." Such an individual could have become a wanted man in many star systems, and decided to flee to a minor colony. There he could avoid bounty hunters and resume his experimentation with a new batch of subjects.

In a similar vein, a **Marshal** could have been a crooked cop in his prior life. Accepting bribes, demanding "protection" money, or using his position to eliminate anyone in his way could have led a lawman down a dark road. Forced to flee or face justice for his actions, he now finds himself with a new start, and a stark choice. Does he resume his old habits, or attempt to rise above them?

THE LOCAL LEADER

Many colonies, especially the smaller ones, contain a core cadre of prominent individuals. These business-people, ranchers, professionals, and other citizens in good standing have a strong influence on a local community. A small colony might lack an established political system or authoritative central government. Instead, these local leaders step in to fill the void,

doing what they can to keep their community running smoothly. Beyond the obvious occupations characters with Colonist specializations could have occupied in a small community, here are some further possibilities.

Most colonies put their children to work on farms and ranches at an early age, but colonies with hopes of expanding their little town into something resembling the civilization of the Core benefit greatly from a schoolmaster. A **Scholar** may have served the educational needs of the youth in a community or collection of far-flung hamlets.

Religion can be a powerful motivating force in a colony, where people find faith a comfort in the face of hardship. A **Politico** may start life as a preacher for one of the galaxy's many faiths. He might be from the bantha-worshipping Dim-U monks, the trendy, female-empowering Zealots of Psusan, the frontier-minded Children of Mani, the serious Order of the Ffib, or one of the chaste Priests of Ninn. Whatever his beliefs, however, he must serve as a shepherd for his flock, and often must deal with more secular problems than spiritual ones.

Many frontier colonies rely on livestock to survive, and use animals as means of transport and beasts of burden. Some colonists keep animals as faithful and useful companions. In these cases, a **Doctor** may have gotten his start as a veterinarian. Tending to the health of the animals in a community may have even led to practicing medicine on the actual colonists, if the need was great enough.

An **Entrepreneur** may have developed his love for wealth and desire for quick riches as a prospector. Precious metals and gems are always in demand, as are any number of gases and liquids used in industrial processes for creating ships, droids, weapons, and machinery. Finding a rich pocket of Tibanna gas or a lode of Corusca gems is a surefire way to amass enough wealth to buy a retirement island on a resort world. Perhaps the character managed to make some initial money, and has now used it to invest in his continued success and prosperity.

The **Marshal** could have gotten his start as the foreperson of a mine or ranch. In this position, he would have to direct and lead his employees, investigate problems amongst the workforce, and even keep the mine or ranch safe from bandits or marauding wildlife. In this case, the character would have to be tough, resourceful, and able to command fear and respect.

Frontier justice can often be as much theater as legal precedent, and for those reasons, a **Performer** might have served as the town's barrister or advocate. Where modern investigative techniques are hard to come by and vigilante justice is a constant threat, defending a client often relies on the advocate's ability to sway the crowd to his point of view, rather than prove innocence with facts.

THE IDEALIST

Many Colonists are exiles from more populous worlds, fleeing armed foes or haunting memories. Other Colonists, though, leave the Core Worlds not out of necessity or fear, but with more selfless intentions. The Outer Rim is home to countless settlements of sentients, and many of them are plagued by political instability, impoverished, or oppressed by local powers. From mining colonies threatened by pirates to worlds wracked by plagues brought by careless travelers, the points of light in the vast darkness of untamed space are threatened by many problems unknown in the Core.

Most natives of the Core Worlds would not consider anything as radical as leaving the comfort of their everyday routines to aid individuals they have never laid eyes on before. Apart from the discomfort of leaving familiar surroundings, the Outer Rim can be extremely dangerous. Still, some individuals feel the inexorable pull of empathy urging them to leave their homes and routines to help their fellow sentients, while others see rendering such aid as a matter of duty, a personal debt to society that must be repaid to those less fortunate than themselves. Each individual has unique motives, but it is certain that there are many idealists to be found amongst those who strike out beyond the Core.

Doctors (or at least those with valid certifications) often receive their training in the Core Worlds—even Doctors who themselves originate from the Outer Rim or other, equally far-flung locales. However, many of those Doctors who leave the remote edges of society to pursue an education later return to their old homes to help their communities overcome problems they could not solve before. A Doctor might return to a colony to research a vaccine for a local disease that took a loved one long ago, help a mining community institute safer purification practices of dangerous chemicals, or simply provide a town with the sort of general medical care it would be hard-pressed to get otherwise.

Entrepreneurs might at first glance seem an unlikely sort to have truly altruistic motives, but the truth is that helping people and making money can go hand in hand, provided one keeps an open mind. An idealist Entrepreneur might see an economically depressed settlement not as an unfortunate inevitability, but rather as an opportunity for investment nobody else has identified yet. For instance, while taking a stake in a failing space station by installing new air recyclers might seem like a waste of money to some, a keen Entrepreneur with foresight could easily help an impoverished community become a hub for local hyperlane traffic—and, by opening up shop there, share in the profits that the flow of passing travelers brings in.

Marshals can have many different driving motives, and while some try to uphold the law at all costs, others are more concerned with the pursuit of justice, for which laws can be both an instrument and an impedi-ment. A Marshal might well venture into the Outer Rim in the hopes of protecting the weak and punishing the guilty without the constraining laws and regulations that might bind the actions of an individual in the Core Worlds. The Empire's rule often puts the law and justice at odds with one another, and when faced with the choice between the two, many people choose to reject an unjust society and find their own path. Few inhabitants of the Outer Rim are likely to care much about whether a helpful stranger had to break a few rules written by corrupt bureaucrats on a far-away world to bring justice to the wicked.

Scholars often make their way into unexplored regions of space in the hopes of learning and cataloguing new information, often to then educate others on the subject of the worlds, societies, and phenomena that they discover. While it can be extremely dangerous to plunge into unknown space, it can also lead to academic discoveries that would never have occurred otherwise. Even a sparsely inhabited desert world might contain incredible biodiversity, with new species of flora and fauna whose unique properties can unlock the cures to dozens of currently untreatable diseases or be home to sentients whose particular technological innovations can overcome problems long thought to be intractable. An idealist Scholar in the Outer Rim knows the power of education, and hopes to discover new knowledge that can help the galactic community at large.

Politicos, particularly firebrands with an unrelenting desire for justice across the galaxy, often find themselves in the Outer Rim seeking to bring attention to the problems that its inhabitants face—problems that the galaxy at large would often like to ignore or forget about. A Politico might approach members of an isolated mining town and urge them to join a galactic union to fight for better wages, or seek to organize protests that raise awareness of the cruelties of local governments and the Empire alike. Some might even openly stoke the fires of revolution, seeking to lead oppressed populations up against whatever regimes hold them under their bootheels.

Performers almost invariably believe in the intrinsic worth of their craft—after all, if they did not believe that their art served some purpose in society, even if that purpose was merely to lighten the cares of others, they would not pursue mastery so fervently. Further, many are not just entertainers, but keepers of cultural history in the form of dance, song, or story. These Performers often travel the Outer Rim to promote awareness of their art and help others share in it and learn about their culture. In the age of the Empire and its monolithic oppression, Performers not only lift the spirits of the downtrodden, but are also frequently the last protectors of precious ideas and art that the Empire would see erased forever.

COLONIST OBLIGATIONS

Colonists have a unique relationship with Obligation when compared to other careers, because they may have lived a long and complex life before becoming a Colonist. Their life in the Core is something most Colonists have simply given up, but for others, it is something they are trying to escape. Connections from that old life can sometimes spill over onto the frontier. Beyond that, many colonies are small, and the tight-knit interdependence of those founding settlers means every Colonist has an obligation to help his neighbors. If one Colonist fails, so might the colony.

Not many sentients born in the Core grow up wanting to eschew modern convenience for the hardscrabble life of the Colonist, and it is a decision each being comes to differently. Consider that even the most famous Colonists in history were probably financial and social failures in the Core, prompting them to board a colony ship for a one-way trip to nowhere. Many might have past debts and transgressions that they will go to great lengths to avoid facing.

Obligations help to define a character and his background while also threatening to complicate matters during the campaign. The hard existence of Rim life is one in which entire populations are just one heatwave away from starvation, one equipment failure away from heat stroke, or one outbreak away from planetary extinction. As such, it no place for further complications from a life long abandoned. Remember that Player Characters can take additional Obligation at character creation. This grants them additional experience or credits, but also places the Player Characters at greater risk.

Players may replace **Table 2-1** in the **EDGE OF THE EMPIRE** Core Rulebook with **Table 1–1: Colonist Obligations**. Players may choose to roll randomly on the table or select an Obligation based on their background. Each character starts play with a value of Obligation based on the size of the character's group and whether or not the character takes on additional Obligation to gain access to extra starting XP or starting credits for gear.

TABLE 1-1: COLONIST OBLIGATIONS

d100 roll	Obligation Type
01-08	**Disgraced**: The Colonist did something shameful, often some social taboo that isn't quite illegal. The shame and sideways glances from peers have forced the Colonist to seek a new life where he can start over free of embarrassment. The isolation of some colonies and cultures makes for some strange taboos not observed by the rest of the galaxy. Thus the taboo can be something terrible, or something as benign as drinking from a public fountain or showing a bare but innocuous body part.
9-16	**Philanderer**: Colonies tend to be small places, and if a being gets around, word about it has a tendency to follow close behind. This Colonist has no shortage of scorned lovers still furious over his or her never committing. Former flames have a habit of showing up at the worst moment, or causing delays when the chrono is ticking. The worst is when two or more flings team up to make life miserable for a serial seducer, or when spouses find out and decide the Colonist is deserving of punishment. Nothing is off limits, as all is fair in love and war.
17-24	**Exiled**: Going up against politically connected members of the Galactic Empire is a good way to become exiled from the most civilized of the Core Worlds. The Colonist is not allowed to set foot in the Core, or on any Imperial-controlled worlds, but is desperate to remove the stain on his reputation. While possible, the smallest misstep can be disastrous, setting progress back months or even years. There is also the trouble of bureaucracy and last minute filing deadlines that can draw the character away.
25-32	**Contracted**: The Colonist has entered into a long-term contract with a corporation or government related to his work at a colony. In many cases, these contracts are how colonists pay their passage to the new world—a form of indentured servitude. Colonists might be contracted to provide bookkeeping, labor, or any number of services. Failure to live up to a contract can result in financial penalties, imprisonment, deportation, or earning a bounty.
33-40	**Bounty**: This is a variant on the standard Bounty Obligation. The bounty may only be issued locally, without the weight of the Empire behind it. These bounties are technically illegal, and attract ruthlessly competent hunters independent of any guild or government. By changing their identity and hiding out in some obscure backwater colony world, Colonists with this Obligation can avoid detection for years. However, the level of violence these individuals can bring upon their town when the truly skilled bounty hunters finally track them down can endanger the whole colony.
41-48	**Debt**: Aside from the running debt most Colonists have at the local cantina, unforeseen financial setbacks are a regular part of life on a newly colonized world. All the expensive lessons for dealing with restless natives, flora, fauna, or environmental conditions on that particular planet have yet to be learned. Most times, the only way to stay afloat is by going to the deepest pockets in town and begging for a loan.
49-56	**Favor**: A colony often begins life as a small community of a few thousand or even just a few hundred individuals. When the only sentient life on an entire planet is that sparse, everyone depends on each other and favors are as valuable as credits. Thirty fellow Colonists might have helped to build a school in town for a Scholar for nothing more than a hot meal, some warm caf, and a favor. This might mean helping get the herd in the pen before a storm, loaning credits, or any number of other odd jobs.
57-64	**Family**: Colonists often book passage to a colony world to start life anew for themselves and their families. For these individuals, making certain their family is safe, healthy, and provided for trumps all other concerns. A comm from home is just as likely to inspire as it is to devastate a Colonist riding herd away from the homestead. Some Colonists have already lost members of their family, and instead are beholden to a final promise, be it to keep the ranch going or take on the role of family protector.
65-72	**Responsibility**: Colonists, especially those founding a new colony, each have a responsibility to the rest of their fellow settlers. A character who is the only doctor on an entire planet cannot simply leave. Even going away for a month could result in dozens of preventable deaths. A moisture farmer's nephew might have a responsibility to keep condensers in the South Range operating, and runaway droids or not, if the units aren't working by midday, there will be hell to pay. The colony only has a chance of survival if everyone does his part.
73-80	**Witness Protection**: Some Colonists never would have chosen life on a distant backwater, but authorities have deemed it necessary to hide them in the witness protection program. The Colonist is being hunted by the Hutt Cartels, Black Sun, the Tenloss Syndicate, or some other galactic-scale criminal organization as a material witness. The Colonist was given a new identity and sent to an obscure planet to safely await trial, but the syndicate won't stop looking for him.
81-88	**Pacifist**: This Colonist abhors violence, either out of a sense of morality or cowardice. Witnessing a violent act can incense or fluster a character so much that he is unable to think straight or control his shaking hands, or simply disgust him to the point that he can't interact with his fellows. If this obligation triggers and the PC participates in a violent act, the GM may add ■ to any skill checks he makes for the remainder of the session. (This may be avoided through good roleplaying on the player's part, such as having his character always try to talk his way out of a fight, and if he's forced to do battle, only use weapons that stun or incapacitate his opponents).
89-96	**Frontier Justice**: Life on the frontier is harsh, cruel, and unfair. Bandits and outlaws can get away with murder and more if the local sheriff is too weak to stop them. Some people are able to let that go and move past it. When the dead are loved ones, however, some can't just move on. The need to get even is so strong it dominates the Colonist's thoughts and dreams, causing him to obsess about the moment of exacted vengeance. The Colonist gladly betrays, abandons, or hurts anyone if it brings him closer to settling the score.
97-00	Roll twice on this chart. Starting Obligation is split into two different origins (this does not increase the Obligation's magnitude; divide the starting Obligation into two equal parts, each with a different type).

NEW SPECIES

FAR **H**ORIZONS introduces three new species to **E**DGE **O**F THE **E**MPIRE: the family-oriented Arcona, the profit-loving Chevin, and the voluble Gran. While each of these species is quite different, each brings unique strengths to social encounters. This makes them particularly good choices for Colonists, and they offer interesting angles for other careers as well.

An Arcona's Vigilance gives him an extra boost as an Entrepreneur or Marshal, and his Willpower is useful as a Politico. Of course, a curious Arconan might find himself forced into an unexpected role when traveling somewhere unfamiliar like the fringe. While an Arconan Hired Gun is less likely than an Arconan Colonist, by coming up with a convincing background, a player can create an unusual and distinctive character. Regardless of career choice, the Mood Readers ability gives the Arcona an added edge in social encounters. This makes them a good option to play the social "face" of a group, if not to lead it.

As a Chevin, a Player Character can be a savvy negotiator during social encounters, while still being strong enough to hold his own in a fight. Chevin often travel seeking credits, and accumulate enough of these to make life easier. A typical Chevin is naturally suited to the role of Entrepreneur. Chevin Traders are a common sight in many sectors, so this is an appropriate specialization for them, and their strength and resilience allow them to become dangerous Marauders. The choice depends on the type of game the party intends to play, solving problems by negotiating or by fighting it out. Whichever role a Chevin takes, he prefers to lead rather than follow.

The Gran are one of the most social species in the galaxy, and a versatile one to play. They make a great "face" for the group in social situations, and their high Presence is beneficial to many Colonist specializations. Gran are a familiar sight throughout the galaxy and sometimes shirk their passive nature, so a wealth of careers are available to them. A Gran Trader with the Smooth Talker talent capitalizes on the species' characteristics and allows the PC to talk the hind legs off a bantha. Alternatively, a Scoundrel is a grittier choice—more combat-ready but still taking advantage of the Gran's innate Charm.

Overall, these three species fit many different character concepts. They have obvious strengths in social situations, but using them with combat-focused specializations creates interesting, multifaceted characters.

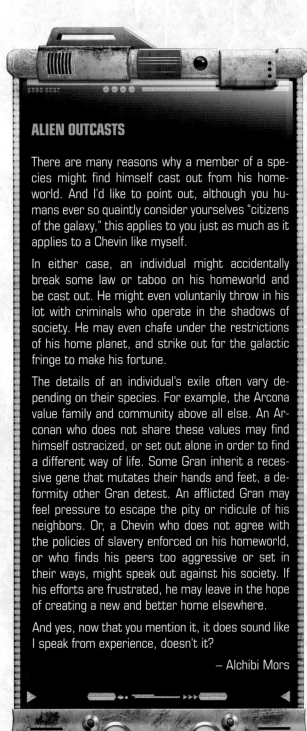

ALIEN OUTCASTS

There are many reasons why a member of a species might find himself cast out from his homeworld. And I'd like to point out, although you humans ever so quaintly consider yourselves "citizens of the galaxy," this applies to you just as much as it applies to a Chevin like myself.

In either case, an individual might accidentally break some law or taboo on his homeworld and be cast out. He might even voluntarily throw in his lot with criminals who operate in the shadows of society. He may even chafe under the restrictions of his home planet, and strike out for the galactic fringe to make his fortune.

The details of an individual's exile often vary depending on their species. For example, the Arcona value family and community above all else. An Arconan who does not share these values may find himself ostracized, or set out alone in order to find a different way of life. Some Gran inherit a recessive gene that mutates their hands and feet, a deformity other Gran detest. An afflicted Gran may feel pressure to escape the pity or ridicule of his neighbors. Or, a Chevin who does not agree with the policies of slavery enforced on his homeworld, or who finds his peers too aggressive or set in their ways, might speak out against his society. If his efforts are frustrated, he may leave in the hope of creating a new and better home elsewhere.

And yes, now that you mention it, it does sound like I speak from experience, doesn't it?

– Alchibi Mors

ARCONA

The Arcona are slim-framed reptilian humanoids with clawed hands and feet. They have compound eyes, which are large, green, and luminous. Their hairless, scaleless skin has a wood-like texture, and green, brown, or near-black in color. The Arconan head-shape is distinctive, akin to an inverted triangle, and tapers into the neck, giving them a snakelike appearance.

The Arcona rely on ammonia supplements while away from their homeworld of Cona, they have poor eyesight, and their claws developed for digging rather than combat. However, they are hardier than they appear. Cona is a dangerous world, so the Arcona are used to surviving against the odds. Their vigilance and adaptability compensate for any physical weakness. They are strong-willed, effective team players, and always alert for danger.

Family is of the utmost importance to the Arcona, and they have a strong sense of community. They often travel in groups, and their wanderlust takes these groups all over the galaxy. A peaceful and composed species, the Arcona are welcome residents on many worlds. Their powers of observation combined with their natural community spirit facilitate social interactions with other species.

Physiology: The Arcona come from the hot, dry planet of Cona, where the blistering temperatures stretch from pole to pole and remain unchanged throughout the year. While they do survive in cooler climates, they show a preference for a temperature similar to that of their homeworld.

The protuberance between an Arcona's eyes is an incredibly sensitive infrared sensory organ, able to detect minute changes in the heat signatures of other beings. The Arcona smell via their tongues, which is why they often expose this slender appendage to the air in a flicking gesture that some other species might find annoying or even insulting. Working in concert, these senses are exact enough to discern moods and emotions in other species.

The atmosphere on Cona contains high concentrations of ammonia vapor. Ammonia produces enzymes in the Arconan body that are necessary for their survival. As a result, the Arcona are dependent upon the presence of ammonia, and when traveling offworld must take ammonia supplements. These supplements must be ingested in roughly the same quantities as a human may need vitamin supplements, and an Arconan can survive for long periods without them (though this can have long term health effects).

Society: The Arcona have a sense of community so strong that they think of themselves in the collective sense. They consider raising a family to be both a duty and a privilege. The Arcona expect each member of society to put the good of his community before his own, and in most cases he does so. On their homeworld, the Arcona live in family-orientated nests, clustered around a Grand Nest where the Nest Leader oversees communal decisions. In families, the males are the primary caregivers, since the females of the species are, by Arconan standards, too flighty and unreliable.

Any Arcona who travels alone, for whatever reason, faces a period of adjustment as he adapts to life away from his hive-like community. Fortunately, the Arcona are ready and able to adapt to survive, as they have proven time and again.

Homeworld: The Arconan homeworld of Cona lies within the Inner Rim. As it orbits a blue star, Teke Ro,

---

SALT ADDICTION

In general, Arcona count restraint among their virtues, but sodium chloride brings out the worst in them. Often referred to simply as "salt," this compound is the one weakness of an otherwise strong-willed species. The biology of the Arcona predisposes them to crave it. Salt consumption causes vibrant hallucinations as well as irreparable damage to the addict's body, and is ultimately fatal.

The Arconan weakness for salt is common knowledge. The golden eyes and unruly behavior of addicts makes them easy to identify. Their addiction makes them easy to manipulate, and ruthless crime lords employ addicts as expendable underlings.

For an Arcona, salt is more potent than any spice, and an addict requires up to 25 grams daily to avoid withdrawal. Since salt is common throughout much of the galaxy, trading in salt is only lucrative for smugglers willing to deal illegally on Cona.

This is a risky business, as salt traders caught on Cona lose more than just their cargo. Arcona who are not already addicts often react vehemently if offered salt, as this hated substance has caused so much trouble on their homeworld.

Salt only affects an Arcona if the salt is relatively pure, so an Arcona can consume salted foods by mistake and not risk any ill effects. If he consumes at least two to three grams of pure salt, he is disoriented for the remainder of the current encounter, and the following encounter. He must also make a **Hard (◇◇◇) Discipline check**. If he fails, he gains 2 Addiction Obligation, if he did not already have an Addiction Obligation.

An addicted Arcona's eyes change to a reflective, golden hue. If the Arcona loses his Addiction Obligation, his eyes return to their natural green.

Arcona

Gran

Chevin

Cona is as hot and dry as any desert planet. It is abundant in vegetation that leaches oxygen and ammonia from the surrounding environment, breaking it down to create water. This phenomenon is essential to the survival of the Arcona. The atmosphere of Cona consists of nitrogen, hydrogen, and high levels of ammonia. Most species require a breathing aid to visit the surface, and even then the stink of ammonia is prevalent.

Cona is also rich in minerals and metals, which has been a mixed blessing for its inhabitants. These resources attracted prospectors and traders who originally exchanged water for mining rights, but then discovered the Arconan susceptibility to sodium chloride addiction. This compound acts as a hallucinogen to the Arcona, and addiction is ultimately fatal. Unfortunately, traders found it easier and cheaper to transport than water, so they imported it, putting the whole of Arconan society at risk. Swift intervention by the Republic and the Arconan government became necessary to prevent a complete breakdown of society.

Language: The Arcona are more practical than proud. Offworld, many teach their children Basic first, even before their own language of Arconese. While most adult Arcona speak both fluently, their snake-like tongues add a hissing resonance to their speech. They

also struggle sometimes with personal pronouns, using "we" rather than "I." This reflects their community-based outlook, rather than grammatical inaccuracy.

Life on the Fringe: The Arcona travel extensively, driven by an innate curiosity and love of discovery. They have spread across the galaxy, often traveling in large family groups. However, since the trouble caused by traders visiting Cona, they have become more wary of other species and fearful of exploitation.

1	2	2	2	3	2
BRAWN	AGILITY	INTELLECT	CUNNING	WILLPOWER	PRESENCE

- **Wound Threshold:** 10 + Brawn

- **Strain Threshold:** 10 + Willpower

- **Starting Experience:** 100 XP

- **Special Abilities:** Arcona begin the game with one rank in Vigilance. They still may not train Vigilance above rank 2 during character creation. When making skill checks, Arcona may remove ■ imposed due to arid or hot environmental conditions.

- **Mood Readers:** Arcona add 💠 to any Charm or Negotiation checks they make.

CHEVIN

The Chevin are solidly built and hard to overlook, being taller than humans and nearly twice as wide. They have large, leathery faces and long, prominent snouts. Their impervious gray skin stretches over thick, muscular limbs, and their sense of smell is refined enough to identify a case of colored water in a shipment of booster blue. Once a species of hunters, Chevin are now renowned for hunting credits, a task for which they are uniquely skilled.

Trade is an important activity for Chevin, whether among themselves or on an interplanetary scale. They pride themselves on their business acumen, and consider wealth tantamount to prestige. Their main exports are slaves and slave-related technology, the only technology they have developed themselves. The Empire is the main customer for the latter. For this reason most Chevin consider the Empire good for business, and so accept and support Palpatine's New Order.

Chevin have developed a reputation for ruthlessness among other species. They drive a hard bargain, and their opportunist natures mean they capitalize on those in need. By Chevin standards, if a colony is willing to pay more than foodstuffs are worth to avoid starvation, the merchant should charge more. If the captain of a starship needs a spare part immediately or risks capture by Imperials, to ask a less than extortionate price makes no business sense. Chevin etiquette demands honesty, not mercy.

In a culture so obsessed by commerce, honesty plays a vital role. After all, honesty is an essential component of trust. Without trust, the trading and exchanging between Chevin villages would break down. As a result, the Chevin moral code requires them to be scrupulously honest, and so Chevin never fail to keep their side of a bargain. On the other hand, they expect the same values to be upheld by other species they deal with, and when double-crossed, they prove violent and unrelenting in seeking revenge.

Physiology: Chevin are strong and tough, with thick hides that are both insulating and insensitive. They absorb damage, and it takes a lot to injure a Chevin or even cause him pain. Few humanoid species could successfully tackle a Chevin with anything less than a blaster. Fortunately, though they are by nature aggressive, given the choice Chevin are more likely to negotiate than fight. They earn more credits that way.

The double-lidded eyes of the Chevin allow them to see in sandstorms or blizzards. They once used their long snouts to track prey, and so their sense of smell is highly developed. Now they are more likely to use it to check the quality of goods than to follow a backshin's trail.

Society: On Vinsoth, the Chevin evolved alongside the Chevs, the other sentient species on the planet. The

Chevin, being more aggressive and hardier fighters, long ago conquered and enslaved their near-human neighbors. Chevin were once hunter-gatherers, but as slavers they have come to rely on the Chevs. Their slaves manufacture and farm for them, while the Chevin have become expert traders and delegators who like to be in charge. Chevin demand respect and thrive in positions of dominance, making them well suited to leadership roles. They have a knack for sensing the potential in other individuals and putting it to good use.

A migratory species, the Chevin live in moving villages, using vehicles called "lodges" to transport their families and goods while their slaves walk alongside. Although Chevin dictators never leave the planet's capital cities, Chevin villages rarely stay in the same place for long. It is therefore is no surprise that Chevin are happy to leave their homeworld to trade, making their home wherever they happen to be.

It is telling of Chevin society that the more aggressive of them tend to rise higher and do better, becoming the leaders in politics and business. However, a Chevin would counter that this tends to be true wherever he finds himself. The galaxy is a dangerous and unforgiving place, and so the Chevin must be strong and ruthless to survive. This grim outlook is a typical Chevin trait, and means that the majority of their relationships with other species are business relationships.

Homeworld: The Chevin homeworld of Vinsoth is in the Outer Rim. The terrain varies widely across the planet, from ice caps at the poles to deserts, mountains, and prairies. Though the Chevin can live almost anywhere thanks to their strong constitution, on Vinsoth they tend to roam on the vast grassy plains.

Language: The official language of Vinsoth is Chevin. Most Chevin also learn to speak Basic for the benefit of trade and travel. They also ensure that their slaves speak both Chevin and Basic.

Life on the Fringe: The pursuit of credits takes Chevin all over the galaxy, and involves them in a multitude of different enterprises and projects. Some travel with slaves, depending on their outlook and prestige. They go to great lengths to realize opportunities, traveling vast distances to inhospitable and remote planets to reach desperate customers, or navigating war zones to smuggle illegal goods. It helps that their physiology equips them to survive and thrive in even the roughest environment. Chevin are practical and do what they have to in order to make a profit, be it smuggle, gamble, trade, slave, or fight for credits.

Chevin have an uncanny ability to find gaps in the market, and a willingness to do whatever it takes to fill them, legal or otherwise. As a result, they often operate outside the reach of Imperial law. There are even rumors of Chevin among the Rebels, though these Chevin invite the disapproval of their kin at home. The Chevin make strong, resilient fighters, and some take jobs as mercenaries. Notably, Jabba the Hutt employs a Chevin, Ephant Mon, as head of security. When encountering Chevin anywhere, travelers should remember that they are better to work with than against.

3	1	2	3	2	1
BRAWN	AGILITY	INTELLECT	CUNNING	WILLPOWER	PRESENCE

- **Wound Threshold:** 11 + Brawn
- **Strain Threshold:** 11 + Willpower
- **Starting Experience:** 80 XP
- **Special Abilities:** Chevin begin the game with one rank in Negotiation. They still may not train Negotiation above rank 2 during character creation.
- **Advanced Olfaction:** Though it originally developed to track prey, a Chevin's keen sense of smell can be valuable in many situations. Add ☐ to Perception checks involving the sense of smell.
- **Thick Hide:** A Chevin's hide is thick and tough enough to absorb some damage, so they start the game with one rank in the Durable talent.

GRAN

The humanoid, three-eyed Gran are a familiar sight throughout the galaxy. Frequenting trade routes and spaceports, traveling in groups as merchants or tourists, the Gran seem to be everywhere. While they can hold their own if forced to fight, these self-proclaimed pacifists are natural talkers. Whether Gran are friendly and open or cunning and manipulative, they boast well-honed social skills. They have a knack for learning information that their source does not mean to give. At some point, most travelers have been the victim of a Gran's friendly barrage of questioning.

The Gran have a strong community spirit and work cooperatively for the good of all. They have evolved from peaceful herbivores; on their homeworld of Kinyen they were once the hunted rather than hunter, living in large groups for protection. However, the Gran have adapted since they took to the stars, sometimes even becoming hunters themselves, taking work as hired guns or bounty hunters.

There are colonies of Gran in many different sectors, as the species has dispersed throughout the galaxy quickly and enthusiastically. The most significant of their colonies are those on Hok and Malastare, where the local Gran regard themselves as natives. The Gran of these colonies have developed different social codes and practices to those still on Kinyen, who consider them only genetically similar. Colonies of Gran away from their homeworld are unlikely to remain a microcosm of Kinyen for long, even if they begin that way.

Physiology: The Gran have a keen sense of sight and can see beyond the spectrum of most sighted species, including infrared. They can also detect minute physio-

GRAN OF MALASTARE

Although the Gran species originated on Kinyen, there are now many Gran who think of Malastare as their homeworld. Their history is quite different, and more turbulent, than that of their relatives on Kinyen.

Once Malastare became part of the Hydian Way, it became a key planet for trading and attracted many visitors, including some Gran colonists. For these Gran, Malastare was a bustling and lucrative planet where they could make a living and meet many spacefaring species without even leaving their new home. However, until their arrival, the sole sentient native species of Malastare had been the Dugs. The Dugs did not take kindly to what they saw as an invasion. Unfortunately for them, the Gran settlers had the support of the Republic, while the Dugs did not. War ensued, from which the Gran emerged the victors.

Eventually the Gran population on Malastare exceeded that of the Dugs, who became subservient to their conquerors. The principles of Gran on Kinyen meant they could not approve of the apparent slavery of the Dugs, or the war that had been necessary for the colonists. They consider the Gran of Malastare to be almost a different species.

logical changes among their own kind that reveal emotions. Gran have two stomachs and digest food slowly, allowing them to go without eating for days if need be.

Society: As a species, Gran are socialists and staunch pacifists, but not all individual Gran practice what their society preaches. Gran have a strong sense of community, and on Kinyen they raise their children for specific careers in order to benefit the community as a whole. This means that while the Gran are not unintelligent, their education can be somewhat limited. The Gran once lived in herds, relying on their numbers for safety. Now, Gran depend on their kin emotionally and hate solitude. In fact, loneliness can drive them insane, often criminally so. The harshest punishment for a Gran is exile, since having to leave his family and friends forever is a fate worse than death.

While most Gran accept the practicalities of their educational system, there are always exceptions. The occasional Gran may find the structure too rigid, and want to leave the planet to do something other than the role assigned to him.

Homeworld: The Gran homeworld of Kinyen is in the Expansion Region. It is located on the Corellian Trade Spine, which is one reason the Gran have spread so far through the galaxy. Many Gran still live in the colorful cities of their homeworld, which delight their keen sense of sight. The planet boasts lush forests as well as large plains of goatgrass, a favorite food of the Gran.

For some Gran, Malastare is their homeworld and their origins on Kinyen merely history. A center of trade and podracing, this high-gravity planet owes its diversity to the influx of species, sentient and otherwise, arriving via the Hydian Way.

Language: All Gran speak Gran and almost certainly Basic, since they love to talk to everyone. When necessary, Gran learn the languages of other species too, rather than miss any chances of conversation.

Life on the Fringe: While not as prevalent as humans, Gran are almost as versatile. Their ability to adapt and make homes and lives for themselves wherever they end up makes them successful colonists. Gran who

travel the stars by choice, and many of them do, often do very well for themselves. Their amiable natures allow them to live easily alongside other species, and their positive outlook can make even the most barren of rocks seem like home. Some Gran even travel alone, but are only content to do so as long as they meet plenty of other sentient beings along the way.

Gran from Kinyen, who are generally peaceful, fight when necessary to protect themselves. On the fringe, where their lives and circumstances are very different, violent Gran are not uncommon. Some Gran do not travel by choice, but exile compels them to do so. These mutants and criminals of their homeworld often turn to drink or spice to forget their troubles, and to crime to fund these vices.

2	2	2	1	2	3
BRAWN	AGILITY	INTELLECT	CUNNING	WILLPOWER	PRESENCE

- **Wound Threshold:** 10 + Brawn
- **Strain Threshold:** 9 + Willpower
- **Starting Experience:** 100 XP
- **Special Abilities:** Gran begin the game with one rank in Charm or Negotiation. They still may not train Charm or Negotiation above rank 2 in character creation.
- **Enhanced Vision:** When making ranged combat or Perception checks, Gran remove up to ■ ■ imposed due to environmental conditions or concealment (but not defense).

NEW SPECIALIZATIONS

The Colonist is already a versatile character to play, but **FAR HORIZONS** introduces three new specializations. The Entrepreneur is motivated by profit and reliant on bribes and payouts to get things done. The Marshal, a dedicated law officer, is prepared to do what it takes to defend his brand of justice. Whether he's a good cop or bad, this character allows the Colonist some strength in combat situations. Lastly, the Performer uses his unique abilities to disrupt and distract, accomplishing his goals via subtlety and misdirection.

Each career in **EDGE OF THE EMPIRE** includes three specializations, which may be selected at character creation as the character's starting specialization. The three specializations presented in **FAR HORIZONS** are also Colonist specializations. This means these specializations may be selected as a character's first specialization at character creation or may be purchased as an additional specialization later on (following all the rules for purchasing additional specialization as detailed on page 93 of the **EDGE OF THE EMPIRE** Core Rulebook). As with the specializations in the **EDGE OF THE EMPIRE** Core Rulebook, characters in other careers can spend experience points to acquire any of these specializations during their campaign as non-career specializations following the rules also found on page 93 of the Core Rulebook.

OBTAINING NEW SPECIALIZATIONS

Acquiring a new specialization is a major event in a character's life, and should represent more than spending the required experience points. A second or third specialization represents a shift in a character's focus, and the development of a new set of skills and abilities. Obtaining a new specialization is a great opportunity for roleplaying, and the choice to acquire a new specialization may be because of events that happen within the ongoing narrative of the game.

Mechanically, purchasing a new specialization happens during one specific moment within a game. Once he spends the XP, the player has added the new specialization to his character. Narratively, however, adding an additional specialization can happen over a long period of time. A character can gradually become interested in a new set of skills that fits into his new specialization, and over the course of an adventure, grow into his new abilities. Eventually the character may evolve into a new role (changing from a research-focused Scholar into a ruthless Entrepreneur who sells the fruits of his previous research for cash), or adopt a role that is a hybrid of his multiple specializations (an aspiring Politico who becomes the elected Marshal of a small town, combining his leadership and law enforcement abilities to rally his community and clean up corruption). It's even possible that a new specialization simply adds an additional facet to an already existing character concept (a Trader takes on the Entrepreneur specialization to further represent his business acumen and success at commerce).

In either case, the player and the GM should discuss how the character adopts this new specialization, and how this may change how the character acts narratively and plays mechanically. These changes may happen in play as the story progresses, or may happen as part of narrative "down time" between sessions.

SELECTING A SPECIALIZATION

Selecting a specialization can represent a major investment in a character; both in XP spent and other opportunities lost. After all, each specialization the character acquires makes the next specialization that much more expensive in spent experience points. Therefore, selecting a new specialization can be a big decision for a player.

Presented here are brief overviews of the three specializations this book adds to the Colonist career, and some of the benefits and abilities each can offer to a player's character.

IN IT FOR THE CREDITS

The Entrepreneur's motivations and strengths are both monetary. A player must be prepared to play a little ruthlessly to gain credits, but also spread the wealth since this character won't do his own dirty work. What he lacks in combat skills, he makes up for in contacts, knowledge, and the ability to buy himself out of trouble. There are many opportunities out on the fringe and the Entrepreneur willingly has a finger in every pie, though he often risks losing his whole arm to do so. He brings wealth to the group, along with all the resources and shortcuts that credits can buy. The Entrepreneur also has a unique attitude towards Obligation, since he has unique talents for dealing with it.

An Entrepreneur cannot resist traveling to the far side of the galaxy if he perceives an opportunity there. Perhaps he has heard that it is easier to make a quick credit out on the Outer Rim. The lawlessness, while adding to the danger, can also suit him if his business ventures are less than legal. Or he might make his living surreptitiously among the Core Worlds, employing the likes of scoundrels and thieves to line his pockets.

LAW ABIDING

Out on the edge of the galaxy, some people do whatever it takes to keep order. The Marshal is a good option if the group is weak on combat capability, since this specialization offers a tougher Colonist than most. His very presence can boost the social checks of an ally and he is vigilant and hard to fool. If the group needs information, he gets it one way or another.

The Marshal is the sort of character who goes where the need is greatest, and he thrives on a challenge. The fringe is on the edge of civilization, where civilized laws mean the least. It is the perfect place for him to make a difference. Wherever he ends up, the Marshal is likely to find trouble. He just can't help himself. A Marshal probably gets involved in situations involving injustice or corruption, and likely drags the rest of his group along.

NOT JUST A PRETTY FACE

Using skills gained as a dancer, singer, or other center of attention, the Performer uses distraction tactics in both social and combat situations. The Performer is not very tough, but is agile and athletic enough to avoid damage in a fight. He works best in a party where there is at least one other PC with a bit of firepower, and helps the group as a whole by distracting and taunting the enemy.

Performers go anywhere there are clients to pay them and audiences to appreciate them. Settlers on the Outer Rim value entertainment as highly as anyone else in the galaxy, though their tastes may not be the most refined. The life tends to be somewhat rougher than working closer to the Core. However, if a Performer needs a fresh start for any reason, or is unable to find work elsewhere, he might well end up in some seedy cantina or working for an up-and-coming crime lord on the fringe.

The Performer could be on the run with the Criminal Obligation, or he might be working to pay off a debt. Perhaps he is just obsessed with obtaining success in his chosen art form, and the fringe offers him an audience that's starved for entertainment.

NARRATIVE BOOST

The GM can use the three new specializations to create new and exciting plot lines within a game. The Entrepreneur is a risk-taker, likely to owe lots of money and get in over his head. He may find it necessary to gather other adventurers around him for protection, or to help obtain the credits needed to pay off his debts. The Marshal might need a party to help keep the peace or restore order in a particularly troublesome colony. The Performer might be on the run from a creditor or troublesome fans, and looking for an escort or bodyguard. By writing adventures for these characters as PCs, or even using them as inspiration for NPCs, the GM can open up a game and give it plenty of potential for non-combat-based encounters.

ENTREPRENEUR

ᚃᚈᚂᚄᚈ ᚉᚈᚂᚄ ᚈᚃᚈᚂᚄᚃ ᚈᚂᚄᚈᚈ

Entrepreneurs know that there is only one thing worth investing in—the future. Entrepreneurs are not unlike explorers in the world of business; they want to be the first to open up new markets, to revolutionize industrial practices, or to create new service industries people hadn't realized they needed, but once sampled, cannot live without.

THE BURDEN OF VISION

Entrepreneurs receive **Discipline**, **Knowledge (Education)**, **Knowledge (Underworld)**, and **Negotiation** as additional career skills. If this is the character's starting specialization, he gains one free rank in each of two of these skills of his choice, without spending experience. While the Entrepreneur is willing to bully, charm, or mislead others to achieve his ends, he prefers to rely on negotiations, bringing to bear facts, graphs, and projections for the future. In this way the Entrepreneur is similar to the Scholar. However, unlike Scholars, the Entrepreneur operates under the assumption that every problem can be overcome with a big enough credit stick.

Entrepreneurs may be free with their money, but they are never wasteful, and they are always looking for ways to cut costs, even if it skirts regulations. Most savvy businesspeople know that if one only plays by the rules, then one can only ever be as successful as the rules allow. Since the rules are usually written by the established corporations the Entrepreneur competes against, he believes the rules exist solely as a means to restrict progress, stifle innovation, and suppress competition. In short, rules were made to be broken. Even the most upstanding businessperson occasionally contracts operatives for industrial espionage or corporate intelligence gathering, and even if he morally objects to that behavior, he needs to know how to defend against it.

It is said that a sucker is born every second, and the Entrepreneur takes great pains to make certain he is never one of them. In all of his dealings, the Entrepreneur must remain vigilant against conversational traps laid by opponents during delicate negotiations. Preparedness is always a part of the plan, so that risk is mitigated and no circumstances result in absolute failure.

Every group can benefit from counting an Entrepreneur among its number. Their ability to negotiate a favorable deal in any number of circumstances, and the resources at their disposal, make Entrepreneurs invaluable members of the team. They make excellent leaders, and any party who allows an Entrepreneur to negotiate on its behalf will be pleased with the results. The Entrepreneur can also act as team quartermaster, outfitting the group with specialized, hard-to-find equipment with little notice, and both his pool of contacts and credit pouch are deep enough to keep the party informed on almost any subject.

Colonist: Entrepreneur Talent Tree

Career Skills: Charm, Deception, Knowledge (Core Worlds), Knowledge (Education), Knowledge (Lore), Leadership, Negotiation, Streetwise
Entrepreneur Bonus Career Skills: Discipline, Knowledge (Education), Knowledge (Underworld), Negotiation

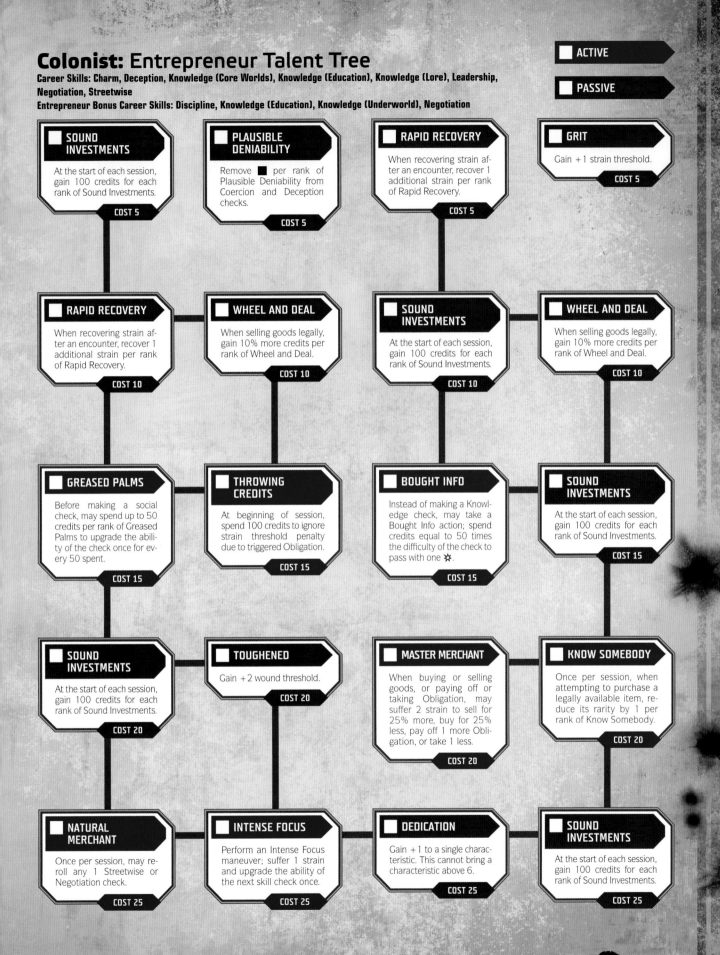

ACTIVE

PASSIVE

SOUND INVESTMENTS
At the start of each session, gain 100 credits for each rank of Sound Investments.
COST 5

PLAUSIBLE DENIABILITY
Remove ■ per rank of Plausible Deniability from Coercion and Deception checks.
COST 5

RAPID RECOVERY
When recovering strain after an encounter, recover 1 additional strain per rank of Rapid Recovery.
COST 5

GRIT
Gain +1 strain threshold.
COST 5

RAPID RECOVERY
When recovering strain after an encounter, recover 1 additional strain per rank of Rapid Recovery.
COST 10

WHEEL AND DEAL
When selling goods legally, gain 10% more credits per rank of Wheel and Deal.
COST 10

SOUND INVESTMENTS
At the start of each session, gain 100 credits for each rank of Sound Investments.
COST 10

WHEEL AND DEAL
When selling goods legally, gain 10% more credits per rank of Wheel and Deal.
COST 10

GREASED PALMS
Before making a social check, may spend up to 50 credits per rank of Greased Palms to upgrade the ability of the check once for every 50 spent.
COST 15

THROWING CREDITS
At beginning of session, spend 100 credits to ignore strain threshold penalty due to triggered Obligation.
COST 15

BOUGHT INFO
Instead of making a Knowledge check, may take a Bought Info action; spend credits equal to 50 times the difficulty of the check to pass with one ✶.
COST 15

SOUND INVESTMENTS
At the start of each session, gain 100 credits for each rank of Sound Investments.
COST 15

SOUND INVESTMENTS
At the start of each session, gain 100 credits for each rank of Sound Investments.
COST 20

TOUGHENED
Gain +2 wound threshold.
COST 20

MASTER MERCHANT
When buying or selling goods, or paying off or taking Obligation, may suffer 2 strain to sell for 25% more, buy for 25% less, pay off 1 more Obligation, or take 1 less.
COST 20

KNOW SOMEBODY
Once per session, when attempting to purchase a legally available item, reduce its rarity by 1 per rank of Know Somebody.
COST 20

NATURAL MERCHANT
Once per session, may reroll any 1 Streetwise or Negotiation check.
COST 25

INTENSE FOCUS
Perform an Intense Focus maneuver; suffer 1 strain and upgrade the ability of the next skill check once.
COST 25

DEDICATION
Gain +1 to a single characteristic. This cannot bring a characteristic above 6.
COST 25

SOUND INVESTMENTS
At the start of each session, gain 100 credits for each rank of Sound Investments.
COST 25

BUILDING BETTER WORLDS
FAR HORIZONS
27

MARSHAL
ᄃК7ДᄐКᄉ

Criminals might run and criminals might hide, but the Marshal won't rest until he drags them back to town in binders. The presence of a strong Marshal is often the only thing keeping a colony from plunging into chaos. The Marshal has a gift for extracting information from witnesses and confessions from criminals, and separating lies and irrelevant information from the truth. Should suspects turn violent, the Marshal is equally adept at talking criminals into a pair of binders or blasting them into oblivion.

THE BURDEN OF PEACE

Marshals receive **Coercion**, **Knowledge (Underworld)**, **Ranged (Light)**, and **Vigilance** as additional career skills. If this is the character's starting specialization, he gains one free rank in each of two of these skills of his choice, without spending experience. Where most Colonists are forced to rely on talking their way out of trouble, the Marshal finds that his blaster speaks almost as well as he does. Most law officers know that holding the weight of the law over a potential witness is the quickest way to modify his attitude. Marshals can throw the weight of their authority around to get answers. There is little government oversight on the fringe, and often a Marshal's word is the law.

Equally as important is the Marshal's knowledge of crime and criminal elements, especially those operating within his jurisdiction. A Marshal who doesn't take the time to familiarize himself with the local malcontents isn't going to be very good at his job. And when it comes time to go toe to toe with those criminals, the Marshal is ready. Most Marshals know how to use the blasters at their hips.

The Marshal makes for a great leader in combat-oriented groups, or can provide some muscle to non-combat groups while still participating in social and investigative encounters. Marshals strike a great balance between social skills and combat, allowing them to speak on behalf of combat-oriented parties without being a liability when blaster bolts start flying. Their ability to sort fact from fiction makes them difficult to manipulate, and their gritty determination can carry an entire group that would have otherwise given up hope of success.

Colonist: Marshal Talent Tree

Career Skills: Charm, Deception, Knowledge (Core Worlds), Knowledge (Education), Knowledge (Lore), Leadership, Negotiation, Streetwise

Marshal Bonus Career Skills: Coercion, Knowledge (Underworld), Ranged (Light), Vigilance

■ ACTIVE

■ PASSIVE

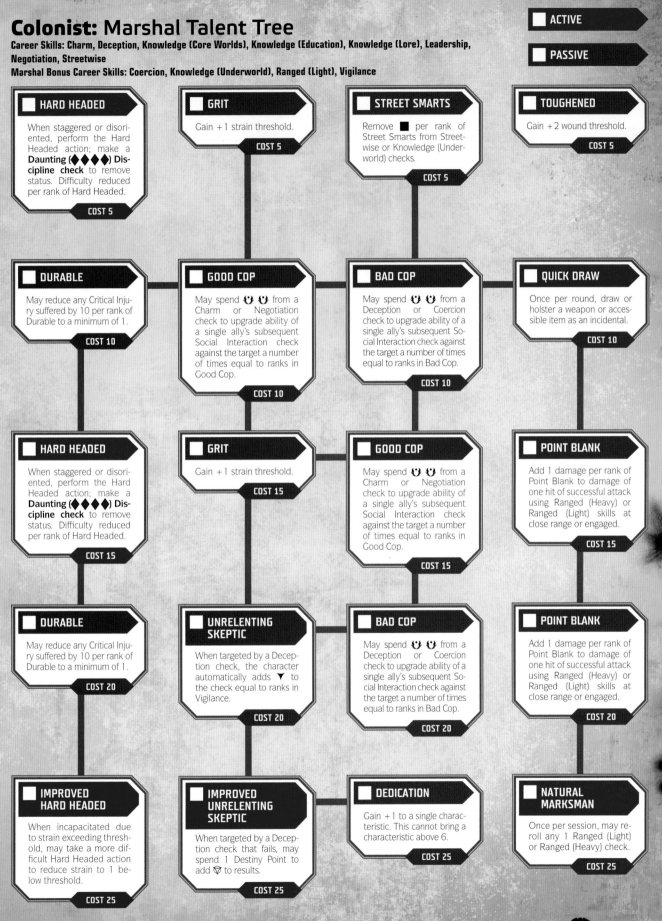

HARD HEADED

When staggered or disoriented, perform the Hard Headed action; make a **Daunting (◆◆◆◆) Discipline check** to remove status. Difficulty reduced per rank of Hard Headed.

COST 5

GRIT

Gain +1 strain threshold.

COST 5

STREET SMARTS

Remove ■ per rank of Street Smarts from Streetwise or Knowledge (Underworld) checks.

COST 5

TOUGHENED

Gain +2 wound threshold.

COST 5

DURABLE

May reduce any Critical Injury suffered by 10 per rank of Durable to a minimum of 1.

COST 10

GOOD COP

May spend ❂ ❂ from a Charm or Negotiation check to upgrade ability of a single ally's subsequent Social Interaction check against the target a number of times equal to ranks in Good Cop.

COST 10

BAD COP

May spend ❂ ❂ from a Deception or Coercion check to upgrade ability of a single ally's subsequent Social Interaction check against the target a number of times equal to ranks in Bad Cop.

COST 10

QUICK DRAW

Once per round, draw or holster a weapon or accessible item as an incidental.

COST 10

HARD HEADED

When staggered or disoriented, perform the Hard Headed action; make a **Daunting (◆◆◆◆) Discipline check** to remove status. Difficulty reduced per rank of Hard Headed.

COST 15

GRIT

Gain +1 strain threshold.

COST 15

GOOD COP

May spend ❂ ❂ from a Charm or Negotiation check to upgrade ability of a single ally's subsequent Social Interaction check against the target a number of times equal to ranks in Good Cop.

COST 15

POINT BLANK

Add 1 damage per rank of Point Blank to damage of one hit of successful attack using Ranged (Heavy) or Ranged (Light) skills at close range or engaged.

COST 15

DURABLE

May reduce any Critical Injury suffered by 10 per rank of Durable to a minimum of 1.

COST 20

UNRELENTING SKEPTIC

When targeted by a Deception check, the character automatically adds ▼ to the check equal to ranks in Vigilance.

COST 20

BAD COP

May spend ❂ ❂ from a Deception or Coercion check to upgrade ability of a single ally's subsequent Social Interaction check against the target a number of times equal to ranks in Bad Cop.

COST 20

POINT BLANK

Add 1 damage per rank of Point Blank to damage of one hit of successful attack using Ranged (Heavy) or Ranged (Light) skills at close range or engaged.

COST 20

IMPROVED HARD HEADED

When incapacitated due to strain exceeding threshold, may take a more difficult Hard Headed action to reduce strain to 1 below threshold.

COST 25

IMPROVED UNRELENTING SKEPTIC

When targeted by a Deception check that fails, may spend 1 Destiny Point to add ⬡ to results.

COST 25

DEDICATION

Gain +1 to a single characteristic. This cannot bring a characteristic above 6.

COST 25

NATURAL MARKSMAN

Once per session, may reroll any 1 Ranged (Light) or Ranged (Heavy) check.

COST 25

PERFORMER

The Performer must always be the center of attention, and if all eyes aren't on the Performer, he has ways to make them shift their focus. For them, all the world is a stage, and the Performer is always putting on a show. They can lie with more sincerity than even the Politico, and do so as easily as if they were running lines for a one-man showing of the Kallea Cycle. They can be as charming as a diplomat, and leave their targets enchanted and completely manipulatable. And far too many people underestimate the strength many Performers must possess for acrobatics, athletics, and even live theater.

right lies to get whatever he wants from whomever he wants. He draws on the best lines from the greatest works of literature, theater, and holo from millennia past, and always has a unique, flattering compliment for any being from whom he might want something.

Other Performers may rely on different tactics in their interactions. A cutting comedian or brilliant actor can hurl a litany of insults that cut to the core of most beings, making them question their worth and their right to deny the Performer what he wants. Unfortunately, these almost psychotic breaks are just as likely to be directed against their closest allies and assistants as enemies. The Performer knows how to use this to his advantage, though, and can create a scene to distract a bouncer while his friends sneak into a club that would otherwise never have granted them access.

However, there is often more to a Performer than just words. Performers may include dancers, acrobats, jugglers, and other individuals who must possess impressive coordination and be at peak physical condition. Their acrobatic abilities can give some Performers an unexpected edge in a fight. In addition, many have been trained in martial arts and the use of stage weaponry for roles in theater or holovids. The agility and overall fitness required to perform on stage means they are often in great shape, and as such, it is not uncommon for the Performer to be the last one standing when the dust settles.

THE BURDEN OF ART

Performers receive **Charm**, **Coordination**, **Deception**, and **Melee** as additional career skills. If this is the character's starting specialization, he gains one free rank in each of two of these skills of his choice, without spending experience. The Performer often leans on pouts, winks, warm smiles, and well timed physical contact mixed with outright

Whether the character is a galaxy-famous magician or merely the member of a traveling troupe of acrobats, the players can build their entire party around a Performer. Performers need an agent, bodyguards, assistants, technicians for their performance, a pilot, perhaps a personal physician, and certain friends or family for their entourage. Performers are able to take the lead in social situations and provide support during combat, but can also take a back seat to a diplomatic leader able to wrangle him. The only downside to including a Performer in the party is that whatever his specialty, he makes his living through some sort of acting. Once can never be sure what a Performer thinks about everyone else.

Colonist: Performer Talent Tree

Career Skills: Charm, Deception, Knowledge (Core Worlds), Knowledge (Education), Knowledge (Lore), Leadership, Negotiation, Streetwise

Performer Bonus Career Skills: Charm, Coordination, Deception, Melee

■ ACTIVE

■ PASSIVE

SMOOTH TALKER
When first acquired, choose 1 skill; Charm, Coercion, Deception, or Negotiation. When making checks with that skill, spend ✦ to gain additional ✹ equal to ranks in Smooth Talker.
COST 5

KILL WITH KINDNESS
Remove ■ per rank of Kill with Kindness from Charm and Leadership checks.
COST 5

DISTRACTING BEHAVIOR
Make a Distracting Behavior maneuver and suffer strain no greater than ranks in Cunning. Until beginning of next turn, equal number of NPCs suffer ◎ on checks. Range increases with additional ranks.
COST 5

CONVINCING DEMEANOR
Remove ■ per rank of Convincing Demeanor from Deception or Skulduggery checks.
COST 5

DISTRACTING BEHAVIOR
Make a Distracting Behavior maneuver and suffer strain no greater than ranks in Cunning. Until beginning of next turn, equal number of NPCs suffer ◎ on checks. Range increases with additional ranks.
COST 10

CONGENIAL
May suffer a number of strain to downgrade difficulty of Charm or Negotiation checks or upgrade difficulty when targeted by Charm or Negotiation checks, by an equal number. Strain suffered this way cannot exceed ranks in Congenial.
COST 10

DODGE
When targeted by combat check, may perform a Dodge incidental to suffer a number of strain no greater than ranks of Dodge, then upgrade the difficulty of the check by that number.
COST 10

JUMP UP
Once per round, may stand from seated or prone as an incidental.
COST 10

DISTRACTING BEHAVIOR
Make a Distracting Behavior maneuver and suffer strain no greater than ranks in Cunning. Until beginning of next turn, equal number of NPCs suffer ◎ on checks. Range increases with additional ranks.
COST 15

INTENSE PRESENCE
Spend 1 Destiny Point to recover strain equal to Presence rating.
COST 15

NATURAL ATHLETE
Once per session, may re-roll any 1 Athletics or Coordination check.
COST 15

SECOND WIND
Once per encounter, may use Second Wind incidental to recover strain equal to ranks in Second Wind.
COST 15

SMOOTH TALKER
When first acquired, choose 1 skill; Charm, Coercion, Deception, or Negotiation. When making checks with that skill, spend ✦ to gain additional ✹ equal to ranks in Smooth Talker.
COST 20

IMPROVED DISTRACTING BEHAVIOR
The Distracting Behavior maneuver inflicts ◎ ◎ on NPCs' checks when NPCs target character's allies.
COST 20

GRIT
Gain +1 strain threshold.
COST 20

TOUGHENED
Gain +2 wound threshold.
COST 20

BIGGEST FAN
Once per session, may take a Biggest Fan action; make a **Hard (♦ ♦ ♦) Charm check** to turn one NPC into the character's biggest fan.
COST 25

DECEPTIVE TAUNT
Once per session, may make Deceptive Taunt action. Make opposed Deception check. If successful, one adversary must attack the character during adversary's next turn.
COST 25

COORDINATION DODGE
When targeted by a combat check, may spend 1 Destiny Point to add ▼ equal to ranks in Coordination to check.
COST 25

DEDICATION
Gain +1 to a single characteristic. This cannot bring a characteristic above 6.
COST 25

NEW TALENTS

Below is a description for each of the new talents added in **FAR HORIZONS**. Every entry includes the information required for gameplay (see page 128 of the **EDGE OF THE EMPIRE** Core Rulebook).

BAD COP
Activation: Passive
Ranked: Yes
Trees: Marshal
The character may spend 👁👁 from a Deception or Coercion check to upgrade the ability of a single ally's subsequent Social Interaction skill check against the same target in the same encounter. Upgrade the ability a number of times equal to the character's ranks in Bad Cop. A single check may only benefit from one use of Bad Cop.

BIGGEST FAN
Activation: Active (Action)
Ranked: No
Trees: Performer
Once per session, the character may take a Biggest Fan action to make a **Hard (♦♦♦) Charm check**. If successful, one NPC of the character's choice in the current encounter turns out to be the character's self-proclaimed "biggest fan." The exact effects of this vary depending on the NPC and the situation. They can include drastically decreasing the difficulty of Social Interaction skill checks the character makes targeting his biggest fan, the fan being willing to perform minor or even significant favors for the character, or the character even becoming a reoccurring ally in the narrative.

At the GM's discretion, this talent may not be able to target certain NPCs whose adversarial nature is vital to the plot, or NPCs who would be unable to appreciate the character's work such as non-sentient creatures, labor droids, and Imperial Stormtroopers.

BOUGHT INFO
Activation: Active (Action)
Ranked: No
Trees: Entrepreneur
When required to make a Knowledge skill check, the character can instead make a Bought Info action. He spends a number of credits equal to 50 times the difficulty of the check and counts as succeeding on the check with one uncanceled ✹. At the GM's discretion, the character may not be able to use this ability if the information sought is particularly esoteric or hard to find, of if the character is in a situation where he could not purchase information (such as marooned on a planet with no access to the HoloNet).

CONGENIAL
Activation: Active (Incidental, Out of Turn)
Ranked: Yes
Trees: Performer
When attempting a Charm or Negotiation check, the character may suffer a number of strain to downgrade the difficulty of the check a number of times equal to the strain suffered. This number cannot exceed his ranks in Congenial. When the character is the target of a Charm or Negotiation check, the character may suffer a number of strain to upgrade the difficulty of the check a number of times equal to the strain suffered. This number cannot exceed his ranks in Congenial.

COORDINATION DODGE
Activation: Active (Incidental, Out of Turn)
Ranked: No
Trees: Performer
When targeted by a combat check, the character may spend one Destiny Point to add ▼ equal to his ranks in Coordination to the check.

DISTRACTING BEHAVIOR
Activation: Active (Maneuver)
Ranked: Yes
Trees: Performer
The character may make a Distracting Behavior maneuver and suffer a number of strain no greater than his ranks in

Cunning. If he does so, an equal number of adversaries or NPCs he is engaged with suffer ⟨setback⟩ on checks they make until the beginning of the character's next turn. The range of this maneuver increases by one band per rank of Distracting Behavior.

The character selects who is affected by Distracting Behavior and can choose to have this talent not affect NPC allies. It may be that he explains his tactics to the NPCs beforehand, or that they know him well enough to be used to his antics.

DISTRACTING BEHAVIOR (IMPROVED)
Activation: Passive
Ranked: No
Trees: Performer
When affected by Distracting Behavior, NPCs suffer ⟨setback⟩ ⟨setback⟩ when making checks targeting the character's allies, instead of ⟨setback⟩.

DECEPTIVE TAUNT
Activation: Active
Ranked: No
Trees: Performer
Once per session, the character may make a Deceptive Taunt action. The character makes an opposed Deception check targeting one NPC within medium range. If he succeeds, the NPC must attack him during its next turn. If the NPC cannot do so, it must spend all subsequent turns maneuvering into position until it can make a melee or ranged attack against the character. Once it has made a melee or ranged attack against the character, the NPC is no longer affected by Deceptive Taunt. If the character is incapacitated or leaves the encounter, the NPC is no longer affected by Deceptive Taunt.

If used outside of combat, at the GM's discretion the NPC can choose to perform a non-lethal attack if the situation warrants it. If the encounter takes place at a party, for example, the NPC may choose to punch the character rather than using a knife or blaster.

GREASED PALMS
Activation: Active (Maneuver)
Ranked: Yes
Trees: Entrepreneur
Before making a Social Interaction check, the character may perform a Greased Palms maneuver and spend up to 50 credits per rank of Greased Palms. For every 50 credits spent, the character upgrades the ability of the skill check once. How the money accomplishes this can be up to the player and GM, but could take the form of bribes, buying gifts, or even purchasing information that gives the character an advantage in the interaction.

GOOD COP
Activation: Passive
Ranked: Yes
Trees: Marshal
The character may spend ⟨advantage⟩ ⟨advantage⟩ from a Charm or Negotiation check to upgrade the ability of a single ally's subsequent Social Interaction skill check against the same target in the same encounter. Upgrade the ability a number of times equal to the character's ranks in Good Cop. A single check may only benefit from one use of Good Cop.

NATURAL ATHLETE
Activation: Active (Incidental)
Ranked: No
Trees: Performer
Once per game session, the character may reroll any one Athletics or Coordination check.

NATURAL MERCHANT
Activation: Active (Incidental)
Ranked: No
Trees: Entrepreneur
Once per game session, the character may reroll any one Streetwise or Negotiation check.

SOUND INVESTMENTS
Activation: Passive
Ranked: Yes
Trees: Entrepreneur
At the beginning of each game session, the character gains credits equal to his ranks in Sound Investments times 100. How this money is earned is up to the player and the GM, and could be actual investments, business dealings, or even a small legal or illegal side business. The GM can also decide that the current events of the adventure may make these funds temporarily unavailable.

THROWING CREDITS
Activation: Active
Ranked: No
Trees: Entrepreneur
At the beginning of the session (after the GM has rolled to trigger Obligation), the character may choose to spend 100 credits. If he does so, he ignores any penalties to his strain threshold due to Obligation being triggered (if his own Obligation is triggered, it may still have plot complications, but he ignores the mechanical penalty). This may represent the character temporarily dealing with the Obligation via a few credits, or simply indulging in some sort of diversion that takes his mind off his problems.

UNRELENTING SKEPTIC
Activation: Passive
Ranked: No
Trees: Marshal
When targeted by a Deception check, the character automatically adds ▼ to the check equal to his ranks in Vigilance.

UNRELENTING SKEPTIC (IMPROVED)
Activation: Active (Incidental, Out of Turn)
Ranked: No
Trees: Marshal
When targeted by a Deception check that fails, the character may spend one Destiny Point to retroactively add ⟨triumph⟩ to the pool results.

COLONIST MOTIVATIONS

Survival is always the first thing on every Colonist's mind—self-preservation, of course, but also survival of the colony. Even the most independent and self-sufficient Colonists need to be able to go into town for replacement parts. However, beyond those immediate concerns, there are often deeper-seeded motivations, things that could explain why a Colonist left what might have been a comfortable life on a Core world.

The truth is that life in the Core is regulated. The most available jobs are in lower management, desk-riding, or menial labor. There are few jobs that allow for much sense of expression or accomplishment. The wide open spaces of the Rim are different. Life is harder, but a Colonist can create something new for himself and his fellows.

At their hearts, most Colonists are creative. The Entrepreneur, Politico, and Performer are especially creative, incorporating art and creativity into their daily lives. Many Scholars use scientific research and their knowledge of the past to dream up bright new futures they hope to help create. Doctors, like Entrepreneurs, are forced to be creative in their problem solving, trying to keep everyone healthy with minimal supplies or come up with new ways to treat maladies. The Marshal, as an individual, can have just as big a creative drive as anyone, but in his work, he first and foremost seeks to create a peaceful environment for his fellow Colonists to pursue their creative efforts.

The following chart (**Table 1–2: Random Colonist Motivations**) can be used to replace the one in the Core Rulebook, incorporating the new Creation Motivation.

TABLE 1-2: RANDOM COLONIST MOTIVATIONS

d10 Roll	Motivation Result
1-2	Ambition
3-4	Cause
5-6	Relationship
7-9	Creation
10	Roll once on each of any two categories

The next chart, **Table 1–3: Specific Creations**, gives the specific results for the Creation Motivation; if a player rolls the Creation category at random, or selects it, he may then roll a random specific Creation-driven result, or select the one that best suits his Colonist idea:

In order to help players make the most out of these new Motivations, here are some further explanations and ideas for each specific result.

TABLE 1-3: SPECIFIC CREATIONS

d100	Creation
1-12	**Society:** Many Colonists don't just seek a new life for themselves, they seek to help create an entirely new form of civilization. These characters are always looking for that moment when they can influence the way a government interacts with its citizens, be it at a town hall or parliamentary building. What kind of society they want to create varies from one being to the next.
13-24	**Homestead:** Independence and self-sustainability are the quiet goals of those who seek to create their own homestead. These Colonists aren't interested in making a fortune. For the homesteader, it is enough to know that his success or failure is dependent on nothing but his own hard work. He desires to build his own home, and run it as he sees fit.
25-36	**Legacy:** Most species in the galaxy are acutely aware of their own mortality. Some come to grips with this by creating a lasting legacy that lives on long after their passing. On a new world, where there are new challenges to rise up against and the planet's early history is in the process of being written, there is a much greater chance of creating or doing something that will live on. Characters with the Legacy motivation jump at any chance to do something that helps their name and deeds outlive them.
37-48	**Family:** Many Colonists come to a new world as eligible single people, eager to learn a trade and attract a mate so they can settle down and have children. This is a humble motivation when compared to most, but fitting for many characters who find it hard to care about events beyond their life on a simple backwater world.
49-60	**Art:** Artists are inspired and influenced by their surroundings, and what inspiration could be better than a newly discovered planet? The open horizons, clear skies, and undiscovered species of flora and fauna can spark the creative impulse in anyone. Some of those on the frontier may seek to bring some art and culture into the new world. Others might seek to support the creation of art by acting as a patron.
61-72	**Cure:** Far from the cutting edge medicine of the Core, the fringe can seem an unhealthy place to live. But many seemingly worthless worlds may hold the key to wiping out deadly diseases. This might be the entire reason a character has chosen to be a Colonist; to save a colony, a planet, or simply a friend or loved one from disease.
73-84	**Understanding:** Many Colonists take an interest in their adopted world, seeking to gain a greater knowledge of their new home. Characters who seek to create a better understanding of the world have an insatiable curiosity about anything pertaining to the planet. This motivation can also refer to creating a peace between settlers, or between settlers and indigenes.
85-00	**Business:** Creating a new business to serve an untapped market is a dream shared by many Colonists. Most of those traveling to a new world hope only to open up a shop where they can ply their trade, but some think bigger. A business started on a small colony may eventually grow to be an enterprise that rivals Kuat Drive Yards or Corellian Engineering Corporation.

COLONIST SIGNATURE ABILITIES

In addition to the specializations that a character can choose from within a given career, he also has access to that career's signature abilities. These abilities are special, elite talents only experienced characters of the specified career have access to. They are feats only possible through the character's skill and ability gained over a long and successful career.

SIGNATURE ABILITY BREAKDOWN

Signature abilities are composed of three elements: the nodes linking it to a talent tree, the ability's basic form, and a series of upgrades that augment the ability.

NODES

Each signature ability has four nodes lined up across its top. These four nodes match up with the four talents on the bottom row of a talent tree. Each node can either be active, showing a bracket facing upward, or inactive, remaining blank. To be able to attach a signature ability to a tree, the character must own all of the talents along the bottom row of the destination talent tree that match up with the active nodes on the signature ability.

ABILITY BASIC FORM

When a character acquires a signature ability, he must first purchase the basic form of the ability. This takes up the entire first row of the signature ability tree, and is purchased with experience points. The experience cost of each upgrade is listed in its box.

UPGRADES

After the character has purchased the basic form of the signature ability, he can further customize the ability by purchasing upgrades. Upgrades, much like talents, are purchased with experience points, and each upgrade may only be purchased if it connects to the basic form of the ability or a previously purchased upgrade. The experience cost of each upgrade is listed in its box.

ACQUIRING SIGNATURE ABILITIES

Before a character can purchase a signature ability or any of its upgrades, the character must "attach" that ability to the bottom of one of his current in-career talent trees. Once a signature ability has been attached to a tree, no other signature abilities may be attached to that tree, and the attached ability cannot be removed or switched to a different tree. A character can only acquire a signature ability from his career, and can only attach that ability to in-career talent trees.

To attach a signature ability to one of his talent trees, the character must own all of the talents along the bottom row of the destination talent tree that match up with the active nodes on the signature ability. Then, once a signature ability has been attached to a talent tree, the character may purchase the ability's basic form and its upgrades using experience, just as if they were talents.

COLONIST SIGNATURE ABILITIES

The Colonist career has access to two signature abilities: Insightful Revelation and Unmatched Expertise.

INSIGHTFUL REVELATION

Many fringers may scoff at the highly educated individual, mocking him as an ivory tower academic with no experience in the real world. What most people don't realize is just how effective the academic can be when he applies his formidable intellect and lengthy education to the task at hand. When confronted with an impossible quandary, the Colonist can use his vast store of knowledge to analyze the problem and arrive at a solution nobody else could have even begun to figure out.

BASE ABILITY

Once per game session, the character may spend two Destiny Points to perform the Insightful Revelation action. If he does so, he makes a **Hard (♦♦♦) Knowledge (Education) check**. If he succeeds, he learns some valuable information that he did not previously possess pertaining to his current situation. What he learns is up to the GM, but it must be valuable to the player in overcoming his immediate encounter or situation, and the information cannot be obtainable by any other immediately available means.

When making the skill check to activate Insightful Revelation, the GM can add ☐ or ■ for any situational effects that might cause the test to be more easy or difficult.

UPGRADES

Insightful Revelation has several upgrades that can improve its effects and make it easier to use. Any upgrades that appear in Insightful Revelation's tree multiple times have their effects stack.

Reduce Setback: When making the skill check to activate Insightful Revelation, the character removes ■.

Add Boost: When making the skill check to activate Insightful Revelation, the character adds ☐.

Destiny: To activate Insightful Revelation, the character only needs to spend one Destiny Point instead of the normal two.

Reduce Difficulty: The skill check to activate Insightful Revelation is **Average (◆◆)** instead of **Hard (◆◆◆)**.

Increase Effect: The character may spend ✦ generated on a successful Insightful Revelation check to gain one additional piece of information. The information must be as useful as the original information.

Duration: The character may perform the Insightful Revelation action one additional time per game session.

Additional Skills: When making the Insightful Revelation action, the character may replace Knowledge (Education) with any other Knowledge skill.

UNMATCHED EXPERTISE

A combination of education and hard-earned life experiences can make Colonists far more capable individuals than they appear. When the time is right, they can put their vast experience to good use, making challenging tasks look easy, and the impossible merely difficult.

BASE ABILITY

Once per game session as an action, the character may spend two Destiny Points to reduce the difficulty of all career skill checks he makes by one, to a minimum of Easy, for the remainder of the encounter.

UPGRADES

Unmatched Expertise has several upgrades that can improve its effects and make it easier to use. Any upgrades that appear in Unmatched Expertise's tree multiple times have their effects stack.

Reduce Setback: When making the skill check to activate Unmatched Expertise, the character removes ■.

Reduce Difficulty: Unmatched Expertise reduces the difficulty of subsequent career skill checks by two instead of one.

Colonist Signature Ability Tree: Insightful Revelation

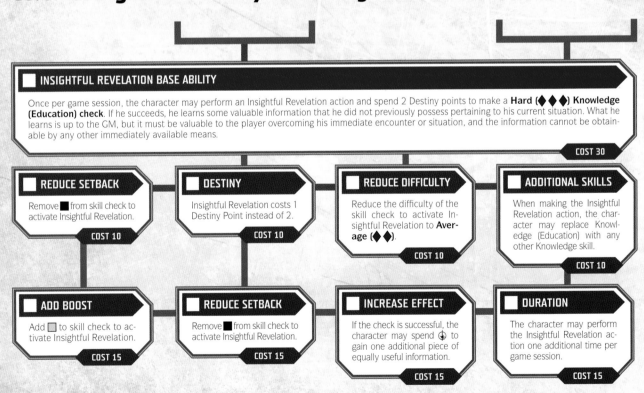

☐ **INSIGHTFUL REVELATION BASE ABILITY**

Once per game session, the character may perform an Insightful Revelation action and spend 2 Destiny points to make a **Hard (◆◆◆) Knowledge (Education) check**. If he succeeds, he learns some valuable information that he did not previously possess pertaining to his current situation. What he learns is up to the GM, but it must be valuable to the player overcoming his immediate encounter or situation, and the information cannot be obtainable by any other immediately available means.

COST 30

☐ **REDUCE SETBACK**

Remove ■ from skill check to activate Insightful Revelation.

COST 10

☐ **DESTINY**

Insightful Revelation costs 1 Destiny Point instead of 2.

COST 10

☐ **REDUCE DIFFICULTY**

Reduce the difficulty of the skill check to activate Insightful Revelation to **Average (◆◆)**.

COST 10

☐ **ADDITIONAL SKILLS**

When making the Insightful Revelation action, the character may replace Knowledge (Education) with any other Knowledge skill.

COST 10

☐ **ADD BOOST**

Add ☐ to skill check to activate Insightful Revelation.

COST 15

☐ **REDUCE SETBACK**

Remove ■ from skill check to activate Insightful Revelation.

COST 15

☐ **INCREASE EFFECT**

If the check is successful, the character may spend ✦ to gain one additional piece of equally useful information.

COST 15

☐ **DURATION**

The character may perform the Insightful Revelation action one additional time per game session.

COST 15

Reduce Difficulty: Unmatched Expertise reduces the difficulty of subsequent career skill checks to a minimum of Simple instead of Easy.

Activation: Unmatched Expertise becomes a maneuver, instead of an action.

Activation: Unmatched Expertise becomes an incidental that may be triggered out of turn, instead of an action.

Destiny: To activate Unmatched Expertise, the character only needs to spend one Destiny Point instead of the normal two.

Superior Reduction: Once per session, once the character has activated Unmatched Expertise, he may also use it to reduce the difficulty of one non-career skill check he makes. This follows the same rules as using Unmatched Expertise to reduce the difficulty of career skills.

Colonist Signature Ability Tree: Unmatched Expertise

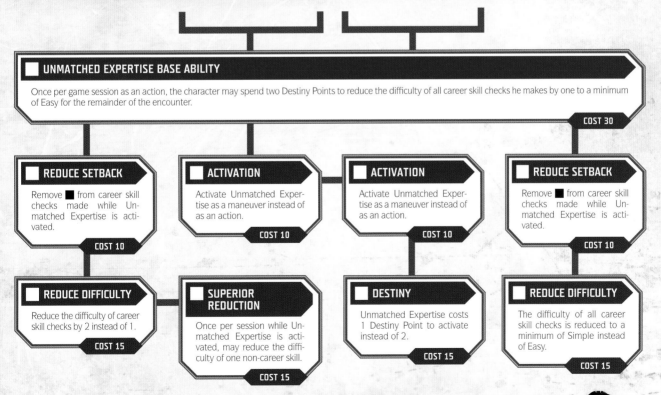

UNMATCHED EXPERTISE BASE ABILITY

Once per game session as an action, the character may spend two Destiny Points to reduce the difficulty of all career skill checks he makes by one to a minimum of Easy for the remainder of the encounter.

COST 30

REDUCE SETBACK
Remove ■ from career skill checks made while Unmatched Expertise is activated.
COST 10

ACTIVATION
Activate Unmatched Expertise as a maneuver instead of as an action.
COST 10

ACTIVATION
Activate Unmatched Expertise as a maneuver instead of as an action.
COST 10

REDUCE SETBACK
Remove ■ from career skill checks made while Unmatched Expertise is activated.
COST 10

REDUCE DIFFICULTY
Reduce the difficulty of career skill checks by 2 instead of 1.
COST 15

SUPERIOR REDUCTION
Once per session while Unmatched Expertise is activated, may reduce the difficulty of one non-career skill.
COST 15

DESTINY
Unmatched Expertise costs 1 Destiny Point to activate instead of 2.
COST 15

REDUCE DIFFICULTY
The difficulty of all career skill checks is reduced to a minimum of Simple instead of Easy.
COST 15

LAW AND ORDNANCE

"In my experience, law and justice are rarely the same."

-Marshal Jacobi Sterne

Typically, Colonists are the characters least likely to embrace violence when other means may suffice. However, it would be a mistake to assume Colonists have no need of arms, armor, and other sundry equipment. In fact, due to their somewhat specialized professions, most Colonists may desire very specific items to complement their skills. Marshals need access to a wide variety of weapons, many of which are designed for riot suppression or non-lethal takedowns. Performers must have all manner of amplifiers, props, or instruments. Doctors require a great deal of surgical equipment and medical supplies. Even Politicos need access to information, and Traders and Entrepreneurs need business aids. And of course, on the fringe of the galaxy, violence (and the need to protect against it) is all too commonplace.

This chapter presents a wide array of equipment appropriate for Colonists of all specializations, including those presented in Chapter I.

WEAPONS AND ARMOR

The galaxy is a dangerous and unforgiving place, and no one knows that fact better than the hardy individuals who make their living taming the edge of the Outer Rim territories. To assist these brave souls in their work, numerous weapons specifically tailored to their needs are available from all major arms manufacturers. In addition, Colonists need to be able to obtain clothing that can protect against the hazards of their professions as well as the occasional blaster bolt. The list of weapons and armor starting on page 40 is only a small sample of the wide array of personal arms available to the Colonist.

NEW WEAPONS

In the Outer Rim, many issues are settled not through lengthy negotiation but through the necessary and violent expedient of the blaster. The following weapons are designed with the needs of the Colonist in mind.

ENERGY WEAPONS

A good blaster is worth its weight in gold out among the Outer Rim territories. The following are a selection of common energy and blaster weapons carried by the rugged men and women colonizing the edge of the known galaxy.

12 DEFENDER

Described as a "micro blaster" in advertising literature, the 12 Defender holdout blaster by Gee-Tech is a weapon of dubious quality and legality. Touted as "the smallest, most reliable self-defense blaster for sale in the galaxy," this tiny pistol is a light, easily concealable, low-powered holdout blaster marketed to wealthy individuals such as merchants, entertainers, and politicians. In theory, the 12 Defender is perfect for those who need a bit of personal protection but have no need or desire to carry a larger blaster pistol. In practice, however, this tiny pistol is a cheaply made, largely disposable weapon of questionable reliability. Produced in the millions and possessing no distinguishing markings (not even a serial number) these weapons feature a ceraplas frame coated with a non-reactive polymer case, which makes them incredibly light and nearly invisible to weapon detection systems. They carry only two shots in their integral power pack, and, once fired, cannot be recharged and retain only a small amount of scrap value.

While the 12 Defender certainly does offer a fair amount of protection for the price, its shoddy construction and lack of versatility limits its usefulness to the average galactic citizen. However, due to its ease of concealment, ability to elude scanners, untraceable components, and disposable nature, this tiny pistol has found an avid following among the criminal classes.

Add ■■ to a character's Computers and Perception checks when attempting to find a 12 Defender on a person's body. The A 12 Defender may not be reloaded.

MODEL Q4 QUICKFIRE HOLDOUT BLASTER

Touted as a revolution in light blaster design, Merr-Sonn's Q4 Quickfire is one of the more unique holdout blasters on the market today. Instead of the typical gas chamber and energy cell power supply, the Q4 possesses an integral rechargeable power pack that provides more stopping power and a higher cyclic rate of fire than other holdouts. The trade-off for this extra power is the fact that the power pack must be recharged instead of easily replaced (a process that takes ten minutes), as well as the weapon's dismal performance at anything farther than short range.

Add ■ to a character's Perception checks when attempting to find a Q4 Quickfire on a person's body. If this weapon runs out of ammo due to a ▽ result, it may not be reloaded by Extra Reloads, the Spare Clip talent, or other means.

SWE/2 SONIC RIFLE

Known primarily for their finely designed skiffs and robust security systems, Telex-Delcor also produces a line of reliable and easy-to-use non-lethal riot control devices. One of their more unique offerings is the SWE/2 Sonic Rifle. A refinement of the SWE/1 Sonic Suppressor released during the Clone Wars, the SWE/2 is a long-barreled firearm designed to incapacitate even the toughest, most persistent malcontent. Using a powerful acoustic generator, the SWE/2 fires a concentrated beam of sound waves similar in power and performance to the particle beam packets fired by blasters. When used on sentient beings, this weapon affects the targets' hearing and sense of balance, staggering the targets and shorting out their fine motor centers. Similar to its Clone Wars-era predecessor, the sonic blast generated by the SWE/2 cannot be parried or disrupted by a lightsaber; a very attractive feature during the end of the Clone Wars, but of limited usefulness today.

OTHER WEAPONS

Many specialty weapons are produced by the likes of Czerka Arms and Merr-Sonn for use as anti-riot weapons. These weapons fire ammunition ranging from rubber bullets, to stunning sprays of tiny pellets, to rapidly expanding nets.

R-88 SUPPRESSOR RIOT RIFLE

Produced by the non-lethal weapons division of Merr-Sonn Munitions, the R-88 is one of the most common riot control weapons in the galaxy. First released decades before the Clone Wars, the R-88 is similar in design and operation to the rare and expensive Stokhli Spray Stick. These long arms resemble bulky blaster rifles with two large cylinders slung beneath the barrel. The cylinders are loaded with a highly effective liquid nerve agent called Brix-C Stun Fluid, which is

TABLE 2-1: RANGED WEAPONS

Name	Skill	Dam	Crit	Range	Encum	HP	Price	Rarity	Special
Energy Weapons									
12 Defender	Ranged (Light)	5	5	Short	1	0	25	4	Inferior, Limited Ammo 2
Quickfire	Ranged (Light)	5	3	Short	1	0	250	4	Stun Setting
Sonic Rifle	Ranged (Heavy)	8	6	Long	4	3	1,200	6	Concussive 1, Slow-Firing 1, Stun Damage
Other Weapons									
Spray Stick	Ranged (Heavy)	0	–	Long	4	0	2,500	8	Accurate 2, Ensnare 4, Slow-Firing 1, Stun 8
Suppressor	Ranged (Heavy)	8	–	Medium	4	2	2,000	5	Blast 5, Disorient 3, Stun Damage
Tangle Gun	Ranged (Heavy)	1	4	Short	2	1	500	5	Ensnare 3

synthesized by Merr-Sonn. When fired, the Suppressor shoots a high velocity, concentrated stream of Brix-C that quickly aerosolizes as it travels. Effective at short and medium ranges, the stun fluid deals its damage either through inhalation or skin contact and causes nausea, impaired vision, difficulty breathing, burning pain, and unconsciousness.

While highly effective against sudden riots or other disturbances, the stun fluid is easily countered by breath masks and heavy clothing. This makes it less effective against determined, well organized targets expecting such weapons. At the GM's discretion, characters wearing breathing gear or sealed armor may take no damage or suffer no effects from the Suppressor.

STOKHLI SPRAY STICK

Designed ages ago by the Stokhli, a non-human nomadic race from the Inner Rim world of Manress, these long-range non-lethal weapons are perfect for crowd control and riot suppression. Used primarily by the Stokhli to hunt the large, incredibly aggressive megafauna of their homeworld, the Spray Stick is a meter long metal rod with a tightly focused spray nozzle at one end and a stun pad equipped buttstock at the other. Fired from the shoulder like a blaster rifle, these weapons shoot a highly concentrated spraynet mist. The mist condenses into a liquid, then into a solid web while in flight, enveloping and immobilizing its target. In addition, as the net envelops its target, it delivers a powerful electrical charge. Extremely rare and finely made, each Stokhli Spray Stick comes equipped with an accurate range finder and a fine aerosol control system that allows the user to more easily hit targets at long range. Despite their rarity and steep price, Stokhli Spray Sticks are always in demand.

When using the stun pad on the butt-stock, the Stokhli Spray Stick can be used as a melee weapon with the following profile (Skill Melee; Damage +2; Critical –; Range [Engaged]; Inaccurate 1, Stun Damage)

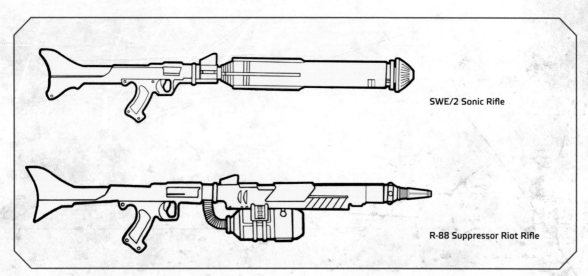

SWE/2 Sonic Rifle

R-88 Suppressor Riot Rifle

TABLE 2-2: MELEE WEAPONS

Name	Skill	Dam	Crit	Range	Encum	HP	Price	Rarity	Special
Brawl Weapons									
Backhand Shock Gloves	Brawl	+1	3	Engaged	0	2	2,000	4	Concussive 1, Stun Damage, Slow-Firing 1
Melee Weapons									
Molecular Stiletto	Melee	+0	2	Engaged	1	1	500	5	Pierce 5, Vicious 1
Riot Shield	Melee	+0	6	Engaged	5	1	300	4	Cumbersome 3, Defensive 2, Deflection 2, Disorient 1
Stun Baton	Melee	+2	6	Engaged	2	2	200	4	Disorient 2, Stun Damage
Thunderbolt	Melee	5	3	Engaged	2	2	875	6	Concussive 1, Stun Damage

TANGLE GUN 7

Another non-lethal offering from Merr-Sonn, the Tangle Gun 7 is the latest word in crowd control weaponry. The Tangle Gun 7 is a carbine-sized rifle with a short, wide-mouthed barrel and polycarbonate furniture that is light and easy to handle. The weapon fires a small pellet of naorstrachem, a sticky and extremely flexible atmosphere-reactive synthetic memory material. Encased in a shell that falls away once the pellet is fired, the pellet explosively expands into a broad, fast moving net upon contact with atmosphere. Once the net makes contact with a target, the being's body heat causes the net to quickly contract, immobilizing him completely. Once entangled, the target must be cut from the webbing. While the Tangle Gun 7 is advertised as non-lethal, occasionally the net tightens so quickly and with such force that it causes lasting harm.

BRAWL WEAPONS

A tense situation can escalate quickly in the rough-and-tumble colonies of the Outer Rim, and sometimes individuals need to rely on his feet and hands to defend himself. In these cases, a bit of insurance in the form of well-made shock gloves comes in handy.

BACKHAND SHOCK GLOVES

Produced by Corellian Personal Defense and marketed toward bodyguards, security forces, and law enforcement, the Backhand series is one of the most powerful types of shock glove on the market. Using an advanced kinetic energy reclamation system to power its high-output circuitry, a pair of Backhand shock gloves gives an individual the power and versatility of a stun baton in a wearable glove. However, due to their power requirements and the nature of their charging system (which uses the movements of their wearer to charge powerful capacitors), these gloves are slow to recharge.

This weapon has the Slow-Firing 1 rule, meaning it can only be used once every other round. This means that while a character may still make Brawl attacks when this weapon is "recharging" he does so without any benefits from the weapon—he simply makes an unarmed melee attack.

MELEE WEAPONS

While some combatants prefer an up close and personal fight, many, especially law enforcement officers, often find themselves in close-quarters combat against their will. In these cases, a stout truncheon, a well-built riot shield, or a well-honed blade often can make the difference between life and death.

ACTIVV1 RIOT SHIELD

Carried throughout the galaxy by law enforcement officers responding to riots and violent protests, riot shields are a symbol of faceless authority and, occasionally, oppression. The Activv1 by Drearian Defense is one of the most common models available in the Outer Rim. Worn strapped to an officer's non-dominant forearm, a riot shield averages around a meter long and nearly as wide, providing almost complete cover for a kneeling or crouching officer. They are constructed from a variety of materials. The shields are typically shaped in such a way as to help deflect incoming thrown objects and stand up to sustained fire from nearly any sidearm, although anything more powerful than a heavy blaster makes short work of a riot shield and the officer behind it. In addition to their obvious protective qualities, riot shields can be used as improvised, somewhat awkward melee weapons, allowing an officer to push and bash his way through a crowd if need be.

Riot shields require one hand to wield, and so can only be used with pistols and one-handed melee weapons. Some riot shields incorporate a slot or mag-lock to allow the user to support a Ranged (Heavy) weapon with the shield itself (firing the weapon one-handed while wielding the riot shield in the other hand). A riot shield with this feature costs an additional 100 credits and has no hard points. Firing a rifle locked to the shield in this way is somewhat cumbersome, and adds ■ to combat checks with both weapons.

THUNDERBOLT SHOCK PROD

A particularly brutal weapon used to herd thick skinned creatures and, on occasion, sentient beings, the Thunderbolt Shock Prod produced by SoroSuub is a weapon with a mixed reputation throughout the galaxy. At once the symbol of bucolic agricultural life and brutally oppressive regimes, the Thunderbolt consists of a solid alloy staff nearly two meters long. At one end is a heavily insulated, two-handed grip and at the other is a series of sharp prongs. The prongs aren't the main threat posed by these weapons, however. Rather, it is the powerful electrical shock generated by them. Able to produce an electrical arc powerful enough to tame a krayt dragon, the Thunderbolt is popular among planetary security forces and slavers, and judicious use of these weapons by riot police can disperse a violent crowd in minutes. The effects of the noise and the crippling pain from the shock quickly incapacitate even the most determined rioters, and these weapons are infamous throughout the galaxy.

MSW-9 MOLECULAR STILETTO

Produced by Xana Exotic Arms, the MSW-9 is a small, easily concealable blade popular among professionals, politicians, and entertainers. Built to resemble a datapad stylus, the MSW-9 is light, inconspicuous, and easily overlooked by even the most zealous and dedicated search.

Due to their inherent fragility, any combat check made while wielding one of these blades that generates either 🎲 🎲 or ▽ damages the weapon by one step as if struck by a weapon with the Sunder quality. Add ■ to a character's Perception check when attempting to find a molecular stiletto on a person's body.

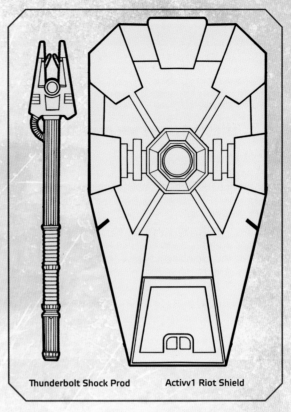

Thunderbolt Shock Prod   Activv1 Riot Shield

Z2 STUN BATON

Resembling a typical police truncheon, the Z2 by Merr-Sonn packs an extra, often completely unexpected punch in the form of a concentrated stun blast. Carried by riot police and criminal enforcers alike on countless planets, the Z2 is a one-handed blunt weapon built from heavily reinforced polymers with conductive alloy striking surfaces. When used against organic beings, the Z2 releases a burst of stun energy that can quickly and effectively reduce a malcontent to unconsciousness. While not commonly used by the Empire, who prefer a more direct and punitive form of policing, stun batons are common in the Outer Rim where law enforcement officers prefer non-lethal methods of dealing with the people they serve and protect.

NEW ARMOR

Despite its popularity, body armor is occasionally considered outmoded by some military thinkers in the current era of high-intensity blasters and devastating micro-explosives. However, armor is still as effective today at saving lives and reducing mortal wounds as it ever has been. Law enforcement officers don specially designed riot armor when dealing with unruly crowds. Merchants and popular entertainers wear stylish, subtly armored clothing and expensive designer armor jackets. Most colonists rely on tough clothing and environmental gear to protect themselves on untamed planets.

The following is a selection of common types of armor worn by colonists and the people who support and protect them and their livelihoods.

TABLE 2-3: ARMOR

Type	Defense	Soak	Price	Encum	Hard Points	Rarity
Creshaldyne Riot Armor	1	1	(R) 1,850	3	1	6
Kamperdine Armored Jackets	0	2	6,200	1	0	7
Reinforced Environment Gear	0	1	850	2	2	4

CRESHALDYNE MK.IV RIOT ARMOR

The Mk.IV Riot Armor is one of Creshaldyne Industries' most popular offerings. Sold almost exclusively to governmental and law enforcement agencies, this sophisticated riot armor is advertised as the final word in protection for law enforcement officers. Worn over a smartmesh body glove woven with foil-fiber reinforcement, the armor is composed of a lightweight clamshell to protect the torso and a number of flexible contoured plates to protect the legs, groin, arms, and shoulders. A blast helmet with a removable, polarized face shield and integrated breath mask completes the ensemble.

This armor includes a breath mask that allows the user to filter out and ignore airborne toxins and gases (but not breathe in atmospheres without the character's required atmosphere mix). In addition, when staggered or disoriented, the wearer reduces the duration of the effect by one round, to a minimum of one round.

REINFORCED ENVIRONMENT GEAR

Produced by a number of companies, such as Pretormin Environmental and Gandorthral Atmospherics, reinforced environment gear is essentially improved adverse environment gear. These suits are especially popular among colonists, who not only must brave strange and hazardous planetary conditions, but who are also more prone to injury from falls or unstable environmental formations.

The reinforced environment suits allows a wearer to ignore ■ imposed by environmental conditions, and also reduces Critical Injuries suffered from falling by 20. The suit also includes a filter, granting □ to Resilience checks to resist toxic atmospheres or airborne toxins.

KAMPERDINE CUSTOM TAILORED ARMORED JACKETS

Kamperdine Clothing Specialists is a small boutique manufacturer of custom clothing items based out of the Core Worlds region. Specializing in the use of fine and exotic beast hides, Kamperdine can produce a stylish and rugged piece of clothing from the skin of nearly any known creature in the galaxy. Their line of custom tailored armored jackets are their most popular and most expensive product. Tailored to each customer's exact specifications, no two of these highly sought-after jackets are alike. Kamperdine can create a jacket to perfectly fit nearly any sentient species that wears clothes, and their client list is a who's who of politicians, entertainers, mili-

tary and government officials, and various other flavors of galactic VIP. A custom Kamperdine jacket makes an incredible first impression, and is a sign that its wearer is an individual of impeccable taste. Kamperdine jackets are rarely found on the open market, and most individuals who purchase one go to their graves in them. They must be ordered directly from Kamperdine months in advance of their desired delivery date.

Kamperdine Armored Jackets are each tailored to a specific wearer. When worn by that wearer, they add ✪ to any successful Charm, Deception, or Negotiation checks the character makes (the GM may decide that the bonus does not apply in certain situations, such as dealings over a comlink).

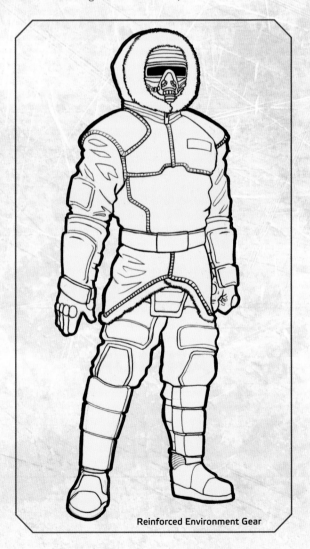

Reinforced Environment Gear

GEAR LOCKER

It seems that every occupation in the galaxy requires a plethora of specialized, highly advanced tools. The Marshal's forensics kit and surveillance programs, the Performer's sophisticated multimedia entertainment suite, and the Entrepreneur's custom light freighter are just a few examples of what is needed to succeed in the galaxy. The following personal gear is designed to assist the various types of Colonist in their day to day lives.

COMMUNICATIONS

Communications can be one of the most important challenges a colony faces. Being able to contact the rest of the galaxy in the event of a serious problem can often be the difference between a successful colony and a dead world.

CHEDAK COMMUNICATIONS X-500 PORTABLE HOLONET RELAY

The HoloNet is one of the crowning achievements of galactic civilization; a nearly instantaneous galaxy-wide communications network. By

routing information through millions of hyperwave transceivers and routers, the Empire enjoys a peerless means of communication.

HoloNet relays, however, are ruinously expensive, and many planets on the Rim must do without. In addition, the Empire regulates the HoloNet and has reserved much of it for military use. However, for those who can afford it, a portable HoloNet relay is one of the few ways a colony can obtain instantaneous communication with the rest of the galaxy.

The X-500 Portable HoloNet Relay allows the user to communicate with the HoloNet (although at the GM's discretion, the signal may be interrupted by jamming, environmental factors, or Imperial interference).

HERZFALL COMMUNICATIONS COLLAR-AMP

The Collar-Amp is a deceptively simple and useful device that is essentially an unobtrusive and very small amplifier. It can be mounted on the user's collar or the front of his clothing, where it looks like an innocuous silver button. There, the Collar-Amp detects the user's voice and amplifies it, filtering out ambient noise. Politicians and law enforcement officials often use the Collar-Amp to address large crowds, while some entertainers hook the device into a larger sound system for concerts or performances at large venues.

The Collar-Amp can boost the wearer's voice so that he can be heard up to long or extreme range (this depends on terrain, environmental conditions, and even the weather). For an extra 100 credits, the user can purchase a model that hooks into a sound system or entertainment system, which improves sound quality.

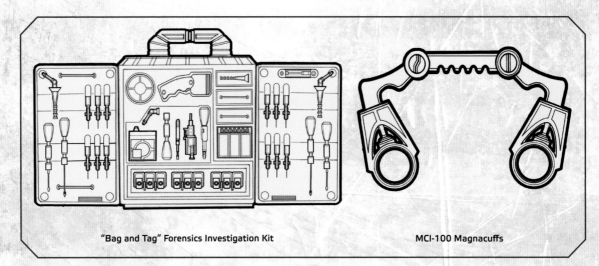

"Bag and Tag" Forensics Investigation Kit

MCI-100 Magnacuffs

SECURITY

Keeping the citizens of Outer Rim colonies safe is a dangerous, thankless, and wearing job. The constant threat from pirates, criminal scum, and hostile native flora and fauna can grind the spirit of even the most hopeful and honest law enforcement officer into dust. To help keep law and order in the wild fringes of the galaxy, numerous companies produce powerful tools to assist the law enforcement officer in his day to day work.

BIOTECH "BAG AND TAG" FORENSICS INVESTIGATION KIT

Essentially a specialized tool kit for crime scene investigations, forensic investigation kits are produced by a number of security companies for use by law enforcement agencies. Whatever their origin, these kits typically contain a number of medical instruments, evidence collection containers, chemical swabs, magnifiers, scanners, multi-spectrum light emitters, marking tools, and different kinds of solvents, adhesives, and specialty chemicals.

When used during the investigation of a crime, a forensic investigation kit adds automatic ☆ to all Perception checks made by the user to spot and gather evidence. It may also count as the right tools for the job when making checks to analyze the evidence gathered (see page 171 of the **EDGE OF THE EMPIRE** Core Rulebook). At the GM's discretion, this item can also be used for related purposes such as archeological digs.

MCI-100 MAGNACUFFS

Produced by Locris Syndicated Securities, MCI-100 magnacuffs are a type of heavy-duty binders designed to restrain unusually powerful or dangerous individuals. Generally built of reinforced durasteel, magnacuffs consist of two full wrist restraints connected by a semi-rigid rod. Instead of crude mechanical locking systems,

magnacuffs use tiny, powerful magnetic field generators to stay locked tight around an individual's wrists, and are locked by thumbprint readers or keypad locks. Magnacuffs can be adjusted to fit most known sentient species, and are popular among frontier law enforcement agencies, bounty hunters, and slavers.

A character may only escape magnacuffs with a successful **Formidable (◆◆◆◆◆) Coordination check** (the bindings on the cuffs are too strong to break with brute force).

SURVIVAL

The pressures of galactic population growth and the unquenchable need for food and natural resources are incredibly powerful, and even the most desolate, far-flung world can be ripe for colonization under the right conditions. It is when a world's environment doesn't quite line up with the physical needs of organic beings that terraforming equipment shows its worth. The following are a selection of complex machines designed to exert control over a hostile planetary environment.

ELYSIUM MODEL 2 ATMOSPHERIC PROCESSOR

Gandorthral Atmospherics is a leading provider of atmospheric engineering systems, producing everything from breath masks and hostile environment suits to massive, city-sized terraforming installations. The smallest of these latter items is the highly respected Elysium Model 2 Atmospheric Processor. Powered by a planet's natural subsurface heat and energy, the Model 2 resembles a massive ziggurat: a stepped, flat-topped pyramid full of systems designed to produce breathable atmospheres, clean water, and even weather patterns from the raw materials at hand. Roughly the size of a star cruiser, the Elysium Model 2 requires a crew of at least one hundred engineers and technicians, not to mention numerous droids to work in areas unfit for

TABLE 2-4: GEAR AND EQUIPMENT

Item	Price	Encum	Rarity
Communications			
Collar-Amp	50	0	1
HoloNet Relay	75,000	15	7
Survival			
Biome Generator	9,000	45	4
Elysium Atmospheric Processor	4,500,000	10,000 (not assembled)	7
FasClean Atmospheric Reactive Damper	200,000	300	5
GX-8 Water Vaporator	2,000	12	2
Security			
Forensic Kit	450	4	4
MCI-100 Magnacuffs	100	1	4
Tools			
Mercantiler Datapad	250	1	3
Musical Instrument (Common)	50-100	1-5	2
Musical Instrument (High Quality)	500-1,500	1-5	4
Musical Instrument (Legendary)	20,000+	1-5	10
Thunderhead PES	2,500	10	4

their organic colleagues. When deployed to a new colony, these processors commonly form the core of the initial settlement, and many a sprawling city throughout the Outer Rim has a decommissioned or repurposed Model 2 somewhere in its borders.

GX-8 WATER VAPORATOR

The most popular and well regarded moisture vaporator on the galactic market, Pretormin Environmental's GX-8 has provided fresh, safe water to planetary pioneers for generations. These delicate looking, spindly constructs consist of a five meter tall tower containing a low-powered ion generator and a powerful cooling system. The GX-8 rapidly cools the air around it, causing heavy condensation that is collected and purified by the systems at the vaporator's base. Once conditioned, the fresh water is typically collected in subterranean holding tanks for use in private, public, commercial, and industrial applications. Typically used on hot, arid worlds such as Tatooine, vaporators are organized in sprawling farms, or "water orchards," where their combined condensing and filtration systems can provide a steady supply of water for a settlement. A curious side

effect of the use of moisture vaporators is the growth of lush native plants and fungi that tend to spring up in the constantly irrigated ground directly surrounding the machine. These small rings, referred to as "vaporator gardens," are good places to collect edible plants.

Depending on the moisture levels in the air, a vaporator can typically produce one to three liters of water in a standard day.

FASCLEAN ATMOSPHERIC REACTIVE DAMPER

Typically found on heavily populated, highly advanced worlds such as Coruscant, the FasClean Atmospheric Reactive Damper (ARD) produced by Gandorthral Atmospherics is one of the most important environmental engineering devices produced. Using a multitude of systems, FasClean dampers are deployed in the upper atmosphere in large groups where they scrub excess carbon dioxide from a planet's atmosphere. This prevents populous, heavily industrial worlds from succumbing to catastrophic planetary climate change caused by massive amounts of CO2 in the air. ARDs are also used in planetary colonization, especially on worlds with a high percentage of volcanic or geothermal activity.

A99 CUSTOM BIOME GENERATOR

Tri-Planetary Atmospherics (TPA) is a small atmospheric research and engineering firm based in the Outer Rim territories. Specializing in atmospheric synthesis technologies, TPA is the go-to company for custom tailored environments. Their most popular product is the A99 Custom Biome Generator, a relatively small, sophisticated device used to create specialty environments in starships, space stations, and buildings. Equipped with powerful chemical analyzers and synthesizers, the A99 can produce comfortable, safe environments for even the most stringent biological requirements. When installed, they are commonly integrated into existing ventilation and temperature regulation systems, allowing the A99 to replicate nearly any biome in the universe.

TOOLS

Every tool, datapad, and esoteric piece of equipment carried by a Colonist represents an additional edge that individual has over his environment and his competitors. The following is a selection of specialty gear commonly used by Colonists.

THUNDERHEAD PORTABLE ENTERTAINMENT SYSTEM

The Thunderhead Portable Entertainment System (PES) is a full suite of tools and equipment for use in the entertainment industry. Custom built to each customer's specifications by Audio Performance Incorporated, each Thunderhead system is unique. That being said, each system does have a number of common components to help the working entertainer. Each system typically includes an assortment of amplifiers, speakers, monitors, sound mixing boards, display screens, light emitters, smoke machines, cables, power generators, data storage units, and other, more esoteric pieces of electronic equipment. The type and amount of equipment varies by customer, but each PES is designed to fit into a single (albeit large) crate with padding and reinforcement

MUSICAL INSTRUMENTS

The number of different musical traditions across the galaxy is truly staggering. From the haunting throat singing of the Tusken Raiders to the cool and sophisticated wail clubs of Coruscant, every sentient species that has ever existed has made music of one kind or another. Along with musical traditions comes musical instruments. Musical instruments are made in a dizzying array of styles, and the list of specific instruments is far too vast to include here (although some common instruments are included to provide guidance), but a character needing to purchase an instrument or instrument accessory (strings, reeds, sticks, etc.) can usually find what he's looking for with little effort on any marginally civilized world. The exact price and availability of a specific instrument not found here is left to the discretion of the Game Master, and the acquisition or theft of a rare musical instrument can easily lay the foundation for a complex and exciting adventure.

Anklet-chimes: These small, clear-toned chimes are secured to the performer's ankles with a length of string or chain, tinkling softly as the performer moves. To properly "play" these chimes, one must be able to control his own movements with the care and precision of an acrobat. Thus, they are often used to accompany dances.

Bandfill: Bandfills are complicated wail instruments, featuring several horn bells. Playing one is difficult, and the best bandfill players can obtain galactic renown.

Chin-harp: Developed by the Weequay, the chin-harp creates music by striking notes with a small chord hammer.

Common Instruments: Most cultures invent some form of horns, drums, and reed instruments as part of their development. While price and rarity may vary depending on the specific instrument, they typically tend to be within an affordable price range, and local substitutes for common musical instruments can be found throughout the galaxy.

Floonorp: Scratch-built musical instruments made out of spare Podracer parts, floonorps are more likely to be

assembled than purchased. The most that can be said for them is that they are both cheap and loud.

Kloo horn: Double-reeded wind instruments, kloo horns are commonly used by jatz musicians and create that music's distinctive higher notes.

MDD-12 "MERCANTILER" DATAPAD

Produced by MerenData to meet strong customer demand, the MDD-12 is a less powerful and less versatile version of the onboard Mercantiler computer system equipped in MerenData's Exchequer series commerce droids. This incredibly useful datapad is programmed with region-specific business information, including currency and credit conversion tables, base value listings for a wide variety of traded goods, and a data uplink connected to a region's stock markets and trading houses that grants the user up-to-the-minute information on all goods bought and sold therein.

When used within the region for which it is programmed—Core Worlds, Inner Rim, Mid Rim, or specific Outer Rim territories—the Mercantiler datapad grants ☐ to any Negotiation skill checks made to buy or sell goods. These datapads grant no bonuses outside of their specific region.

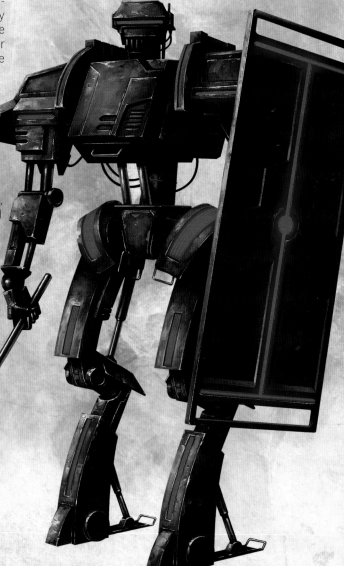

TABLE 2-5: DROIDS

Droid Type	Price	Rarity
AC Series LE Droid	(R) 9,600	5
DZ-70 Fugitive Tracker	(R) 9,800	4
Gyrowheel 1.42.08	6,500	4
Mini-Med	900	3
SDMN Session Droid	4,000	5

DROIDS

In the Outer Rim, perhaps even more so than in other areas of the galaxy, droids are essential to the day-to-day functions of civil society. In a region where so many systems remain uncharted and unknown dangers can reside in even the most welcoming paradise, droids help make life easier and safer for their organic masters, colleagues, and friends. The following are a sampling of specialty droids common in the Outer Rim.

AC LAW ENFORCEMENT DROID [RIVAL]

The Rim Securities AC Law Enforcement Droids are a relatively new entry to the field of police automata, envisioned as direct competitors to both Cybot Galactica's HXZ-1 series and SoroSuub's recently released 501-Z series LEO droid. Nearly two meters tall, these broad shouldered humanoid droids are of average intelligence and possessed of a stern, imposing disposition. Programmed for both standard policing as well as fast response riot control duties, AC series droids are covered in imposing plate armor. Their heads have a single horizontal red band for a photoreceptor and they have only the merest hint of other facial features. Their personality matrix seems to have been programmed with the essence of every hard-nosed, uncompromising, "strike first and ask questions later" law officer in history. They are loud, brash, and skilled at physical intimidation. Their grating manner and their tendency to use overwhelming force in inappropriate situations has led to numerous complaints against both the droids and Rim Securities. While civilians may despise the AC series droids, law enforcement agencies throughout the Outer Rim love them for their brutal efficiency, and they are slowly cornering the market for police droids at the edge of the galaxy.

Skills: Coercion 2, Discipline 2, Melee 2, Piloting (Planetary) 2, Streetwise 3, Vigilance 3.

Talents: Nobody's Fool 1 (the difficulty of any Charm, Coercion, or Deception checks made against the droid are upgraded once).

Abilities: None.

Equipment: Stun baton (Melee; Damage 5; Critical 6; Range [Engaged]; Disorient 2, Stun Damage), riot shield (Melee; Damage 3; Critical 6; Range [Engaged]; Cumbersome 3, Defensive 2, Deflection 2, Disorient 1), binders, built-in comlink.

DZ-70 FUGITIVE TRACKER DROID (RIVAL)

The DZ-70 by Arakyd Industries is one of the most popular tracking droids on the market today. Used by militaries and law enforcement agencies throughout the galaxy, these small droids are not particularly bright but are expert trackers and are incredibly persistent in the pursuit of a target. Around two meters across, the DZ-70 is a small, spherical droid equipped with a powerful repulsorlift system that provides excellent agility and overland speed. The droid's hull is studded with photoreceptors and assorted sensors that give it an unrestricted, 360 degree view of its surroundings. Two powerful, retractable claws are housed in covered bays along the droid's bottom, and it carries a blaster pistol and ion blaster as standard armament. While quite competent despite its low intelligence, a DZ-70's natural zeal and tenaciousness may occasionally lead to the development of an "at all costs" mentality if the droid isn't given proper maintenance and regular memory wipes. This means that the droid does everything in its power, including the use of lethal force, to bring a fugitive to justice.

Skills: Ranged (Light) 2, Stealth 2, Survival 3, Vigilance 2.

Talents: Adversary 1 (upgrade all combat checks targeting this character once), Expert Tracker 2 (Remove ■ ■ from checks to find or follow tracks. Survival checks made to track targets take 50% less time than normal).

Abilities: None.

Equipment: Blaster Pistol (Ranged [Light]; Damage 6; Critical 3; Range [Medium]; Stun Setting), Ionization Blaster (Ranged [Light]; Damage 10; Critical 5; Range [Short]; Disorient 5, Stun Damage [Droid Only]).

MEDTECH MINI-MED (MINION)

The Mini-Med is less a droid and more of a skilled set of surgeon's tools. Designed specifically to aid sapient doctors, the Mini-Med is a small, spherical droid with five spindly legs that can double as manipulators. It cannot perform any sort of operations on its own, but when working under the direction of a talented doctor, a team of Mini-Meds can greatly enhance his abilities. However, their almost spider-like appearance has guaranteed they've not caught on in galactic society. Even pragmatic doctors tend to use them only when the patient is anesthetized.

BRAWN	AGILITY	INTELLECT	CUNNING	WILLPOWER	PRESENCE
1	1	1	1	1	0

SOAK VALUE	W. THRESHOLD	M/R DEFENSE
2	1	0 | 0

Skills: None.
Talents: None.
Abilities: Surgeon's Aid (When a minion group of one or more Mini-Meds performs the Assist maneuver to help a character with a Medicine check, that character counts as having + 1 rank in the Surgeon talent per Mini-Med in the group.) Silhouette 0.
Equipment: None.

GYROWHEEL 1.42.08-SERIES RECYCLING DROID (MINION)

A relatively common sight aboard colony ships and in the streets and alleys of countless settlements, Veril Line Systems' Gyrowheel series recycling droid is, in its way, perhaps the most useful and important droid a colony can possess. Using a powerful cocktail of natural and artificial enzymes contained within their bodies, these droids turn garbage, food scraps, and other organic refuse into a nourishing nutrient sludge that can make up the large part of many a colonist's daily caloric intake.

Standing around two meters high, these hard working droids consist of a broad, round body like a high-walled serving platter around 2.5 meters across covered by a retractable clamshell cover. Dexterous manipulator arms ring the droid's body, and a dull red photoreceptor constantly scans its surroundings for trash. The droid's body is perched on a single hard rubber wheel and is kept balanced by a sophisticated gyro-stabilization system. More a remote than an actual sentient droid, these extremely dim-witted constructs are devoid of individual personality beyond a desire to hunt trash. They operate in packs, scouring their surroundings for organic refuse under the command of a central monitoring computer system.

BRAWN	AGILITY	INTELLECT	CUNNING	WILLPOWER	PRESENCE
3	3	0	1	1	1

SOAK VALUE	W. THRESHOLD	M/R DEFENSE
4	4	0 | 0

Skills: Athletics, Coordination (Group Only).
Talents: None.
Abilities: None.
Equipment: Cleaning devices, grabber claws.

SDMN SERIES SESSION DROID [RIVAL]

The SDMN "Side Man" series entertainment droids were designed by Cybot Galactica to be the ultimate entertainer's sidekick. Designed by focus group and committee, the Side Man droids are built to be as inoffensive and engaging as droid technology allows. They can be ordered from the factory with a number of add-ons and special programs tailored to their owner's particular needs, from an illusionist's assistant to a wail band's percussionist. A Side Man has an obsequious, eager to please personality that professional entertainers tend to find incredibly irritating. As such, most SDMN droids working throughout the galaxy, especially those owned by musicians, have been reprogrammed to be both more enjoyable to be around and better suited to operating in the often seedy, disreputable trenches of the galactic entertainment industry. Despite their built-in personality flaws, Side Men are quite competent and are in high demand by professional and aspiring entertainers.

BRAWN	AGILITY	INTELLECT	CUNNING	WILLPOWER	PRESENCE
1	2	2	2	1	3

SOAK VALUE	W. THRESHOLD	M/R DEFENSE
3	7	0 | 0

Skills: Charm 2, Cool 2, Computers 2, Coordination 2, Deception 2.
Talents: Plausible Deniability 1 (remove ■ from all Coercion and Deception checks made by the character), Smooth Talker (Charm) 2 (character may spend ⬡ to gain ✴ ✴ to any Charm check).
Abilities: Backup Entertainer (When a SDMN Session Droid performs the Assist maneuver to help a character make a check as part of a performance, that character adds automatic ۞ ۞ to the results instead of the usual benefits).
Equipment: None.

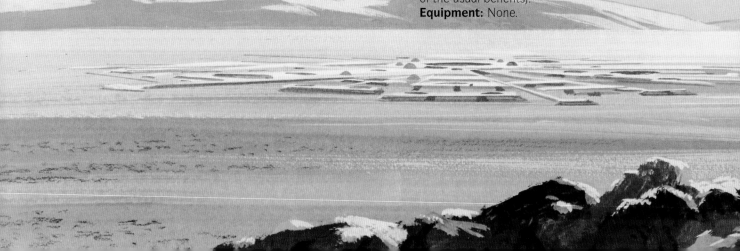

EXPANDED VEHICLES

It is a commonly held belief that the various worlds of the Outer Rim is where old vehicles go to die. Indeed, throughout the region many speeders and groundcars can be found running smoothly and kept alive with love, ingenuity, and improvised parts long after they would have been scrapped in the more civilized, affluent areas of the galaxy.

No amount of preparation, innate skill, or specialty equipment can make a difference in an endeavor if an individual and his equipment can't get where they need to go. Starships, speeders, and walkers are every bit as important to galactic colonization as the colonists themselves. The following section contains a variety of ships and vehicles tailored to the needs of the hardy colonists of the Outer Rim.

AIRSPEEDERS

Many Colonists find airspeeders extremely useful—especially those involved in law enforcement. A patrol officer in an airspeeder can cover wide swaths of territory, which is a particular advantage in rural or wilderness areas. In addition, most airspeeders have the speed to chase down even the fastest malcontents.

MAULER TACTICAL RESPONDER

Sienar Fleet Systems' Mauler airspeeder is a fast, lightweight troop carrier and gunship marketed to law enforcement agencies and private security companies. Based on the design of the rugged Republic Police Gunship, itself a stripped down version of Rothana Heavy Engineering's LAAT/i Attack Gunship, the Mauler is designed to carry two squads of law enforcement officers or an equivalent amount of cargo into a conflict then retreat to altitude and provide air support to officers on the ground. Maulers are popular in the Outer Rim. In addition to law enforcement, they are also used as search and rescue vehicles, heavy pursuit,

and even as cargo lifters if need be. Many colonies possess at least one of these vehicles, using them as all-purpose heavy-duty utility airspeeders.

Maulers are tall, long, narrow bodied airspeeders with blunt noses and tapered rear hulls that bear a passing resemblance to the Imperial Navy's TIE/ln starfighter. A hexagonal viewport of reinforced transparisteel protects the pilot and gunner and affords them an expansive view of their surroundings. A large hatch is located on each side of the Mauler for loading and unloading of crew and passengers, and a drop-down ramp at the rear of the vehicle allows all passengers to disembark quickly in combat or emergency situations. Although Maulers are neither as heavily armored nor as heavily armed as their military forebears, they still have a respectable amount of armor and a pair of blaster cannons.

4	2	0	DEF: FORE/PORT/STARBOARD/AFT				ARMOR
SILHOUETTE	SPEED	HANDLING	0	-	-	0	2
			HT THRESHOLD			SS THRESHOLD	
			20			15	

Vehicle Type/Model: Airspeeder/Mauler TR.
Manufacturer: Sienar Fleet Systems.
Maximum Altitude: 200 kilometers.
Sensor Range: Short.
Crew: One pilot, one co-pilot/gunner.
Encumbrance Capacity: 12.
Passenger Capacity: 24.
Price/Rarity: 76,000 credits/(R)6.
Customization Hard Points: 2.
Weapons: Two Forward Turret Mounted Light Blaster Cannons (Fire Arc Forward and Port *or* Forward and Starboard; Damage 5; Critical 3; Range [Close]).

LANDSPEEDERS

As common in the Outer Rim territories as they are in more civilized places, landspeeders are perhaps the hardest working, most versatile vehicles in the galaxy. From heavy hauling to cargo shuttling to chasing down lawbreakers, landspeeders are nearly always the answer to the question, "How do we get there?"

V-35 COURIER LANDSPEEDER

The sleek and angular V-35 Courier is one of Soro-Suub's more popular landspeeders. This small, coupe-styled speeder seats three in relative comfort in a sealed, well-appointed cockpit. The forward hull is a sharply tapering, wedge-shaped compartment dominated by a seven section, auto-tinting transparisteel canopy that offers outstanding visibility for both driver and passengers. The rear of the vehicle houses one of SoroSuub's SS80 Dynamo power generators driving a MagLift repulsorlift engine. Forward thrust is provided by three Mk.4 LoFlow cluster turbines mounted in dorsal nacelles at the very rear.

Despite its aggressive styling, which takes its cues both from starfighter design and the design of Soro-Suub's racing landspeeders, the Courier is not a high-performance vehicle. In fact, underneath all of the knife-edge body panels and glossy paint is a staid, reliable vehicle with respectable but not outstanding performance that is perfect for a small family or business.

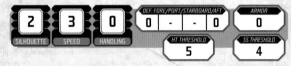

Vehicle Type/Model: Landspeeder/V-35 Courier.
Manufacturer: SoroSuub.
Maximum Altitude: 1 meter.
Sensor Range: Close.
Crew: One pilot.
Encumbrance Capacity: 20.
Passenger Capacity: 3.
Price/Rarity: 7,500 credits/2.
Customization Hard Points: 3.
Weapons: None.

SUPERHAUL MODEL II CARGO SKIFF

Used in numerous commercial and industrial applications, Ubrikkian Industries' SuperHaul II is a sturdy and reliable workhorse of a vehicle. An extremely simple vehicle to operate and maintain, the SuperHaul II is a common sight in spaceports and warehouses all across the galaxy. The SuperHaul II has a single, open-topped deck surrounded by a stout safety rail and equipped with a number of tie-down points, cam locks, and magnetic fastening plates for securing different types of cargo. Mounted in small nacelles on the port and star-board sides of the SuperHaul II are small, low powered magnetic cargo lifters, similar in operation to tractor beams, that are controlled from the operator's station. These cargo lifters allow a single individual to load, organize, and unload cargo without additional help, thus streamlining and speeding up work flows.

Lifting power is provided by a UB-911 Sampson Heavy Cargo Lift repulsor drive powered by a high-output power generator. The SuperHaul II's maneuverability, such as it is, is provided by a number of small, variable vector maneuvering thrusters scattered about the hull, along with two stabilizers located at the aft of the vehicle. Along with a respectable cargo capacity and a reputation for solid construction, the SuperHaul II is also easily modified to better cope with local planetary conditions. Foreign object filters for air intakes, rain shields, light armor, environmentally sealed decks, and light mounted weapons are all offered as options directly from Ubrikkian or from numerous aftermarket suppliers.

Vehicle Type/Model: Cargo Skiff/SuperHaul II.
Manufacturer: Ubrikkian Industries.
Maximum Altitude: 50 meters.
Sensor Range: Close.
Crew: One pilot.
Encumbrance Capacity: 80.
Passenger Capacity: 8 (without cargo).
Price/Rarity: 8,000 credits/3.
Customization Hard Points: 2.
Weapons: None.

PANTHER POLICE INTERCEPTOR

Perhaps the most popular and iconic police vehicle in the galaxy, the Panther Police Interceptor is one of SoroSuub's best selling vehicles. Derived from the civilian market P71 Sport Speeder, the Panther is a dedicated law enforcement speeder featuring more powerful engines, a higher output power generator, and improved handling and sensors. Sold in bulk lots to police forces throughout the galaxy, the Panther is a common sight both in teeming mega cities and backwater Outer Rim colony worlds.

The vehicle itself is a small, wedge-shaped speeder with twin side by side bubble canopies covering the pilot's and co-pilot's compartments. Behind the crew, separated by a thick wall of transparisteel, is a passenger compartment that can hold two human-sized prisoners cuffed to a thick durasteel restraining bar. At the rear of the vehicle, in external side-mounted nacelles, are a quartet of powerful drive thrusters that give the Panther incredible straight-line speed, a useful feature in a speeder chase. Panthers carry no mounted weapon systems, but are equipped with good sensors, a pod-mounted searchlight, long-range comlinks, and integrated datapads permanently synced to the police force's criminal database. A few of these capable speeders find their way into the civilian used speeder market where they are instantly snapped up by commercial transportation companies, taxi services, and hot-rodders.

Vehicle Type/Model: Landspeeder/Panther.
Manufacturer: SoroSuub Corporation.
Maximum Altitude: 10 meters.
Sensor Range: Short.
Crew: One pilot.
Encumbrance Capacity: 20.
Passenger Capacity: One passenger, two suspects.
Price/Rarity: 11,000 credits/(R) 4.
Customization Hard Points: 3.
Weapons: None.

WHEELED AND TRACKED VEHICLES

As slugthrowers are to blasters, so wheeled and tracked vehicles are to repulsorlift vehicles. Sturdy, simple, and cheap to maintain, these primitive machines are often found in the Outer Rim where landspeeders can't survive due to parts scarcity, general poverty, or adverse environmental conditions.

I-C2 CIVIL-INDUSTRIAL DROID

Produced by Veril Line Systems for use in the construction and civil engineering fields, the I-C2 is the latest in a long line of autonomous construction and fabrication droids. Designed to replace the towering, dim-witted but reliable EVS construction droid, the I-C2 is a massive, slow moving vehicle similar in size and shape to the ancient CMC Digger-Crawlers. Commonly found building far flung Outer Rim colonies or performing massive construction projects on heavily populated worlds, these droids are long, stoutly built, slab-sided affairs propelled by massive independently suspended tread arrays. They are equipped with a versatile fabricating furnace that can produce finished building materials from raw materials, and countless retractable building, lifting, and fabricating appendages. The droid brain that controls the majority of the I-C2's systems is highly intelligent and analytical, programmed for engineering and construction expertise with powerful analysis and problem solving sub-routines. In terms of personality, I-C2 droids tend to be slow and methodical individuals who speak in an impenetrable mix of technical lingo and jargon, when they bother to speak

at all. In addition to the droid operator, a small crew of engineers and technicians are assigned to each vehicle, keeping an eye on the simpler propulsion, power, and control systems while the droid does the heavy intellectual lifting and actual construction.

I-C2 CIVIL-INDUSTRIAL DROID PROFILE [RIVAL]

Skills: Computers 2, Knowledge (Education) 3, Knowledge (Civil Engineering) 3, Piloting (Planetary) 2.
Talents: None.
Abilities: None.

I-C2 CIVIL-INDUSTRIAL VEHICLE PROFILE

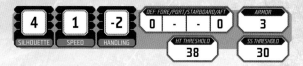

Vehicle Type/Model: Droid Operated Civil Engineering Vehicle/I-C2.
Manufacturer: Veril Line Systems.
Sensor Range: Close.
Crew: None (droid operated).
Encumbrance Capacity: 200.
Passenger Capacity: Six engineers.
Price/Rarity: 1,700,000 credits/6.
Customization Hard Points: 1.
Weapons: None.

WALKERS

A highly effective compromise between landspeeders and vehicles with more primitive drivetrains like groundcars and tracked tanks, walkers are incredibly versatile vehicles used in nearly every occupation from exploration to construction to combat.

ALL TERRAIN RIOT CONTROL TRANSPORT

First introduced in 19 BBY, the AT-RCT is a small, two-man, open-topped walker used by Imperial police forces as a crowd control and anti-riot vehicle. Twice as tall as a man, the AT-RCT is a fast, heavily armored walker based on the AT-RT reconnaissance walker used by the Grand Army of the Republic. These agile all-terrain walkers can maneuver quickly and easily through urban environments and thanks to a specially designed gyro-stabilization system, they can traverse broken ground and barricades with remarkable ease. The light durasteel armor that protects the walkers' delicate inner workings is designed with numerous slopes and complex angles to deflect incoming ordnance and blaster fire. These walkers mount a twin linked blaster cannon in the front of the hull, and two sets of twin linked suppression cannons on articulated arms mounted to the port and starboard sides. Although they are mainly used by Imperial police forces, many planetary and system governments field a handful of these powerful walkers to keep their citizens in line.

3	2	0	DEF: FORE/PORT/STARBOARD/AFT		ARMOR
SILHOUETTE	SPEED	HANDLING	0 - - 0		3
			HT THRESHOLD	SS THRESHOLD	
			8	8	

Vehicle Type/Model: Walker/AT-RCT.
Manufacturer: Kuat Drive Yards.
Sensor Range: Close.
Crew: One pilot, one co-pilot/gunner.
Encumbrance Capacity: 10.
Passenger Capacity: None.
Price/Rarity: 35,000 credits/(R)7.
Customization Hard Points: 2.
Weapons: Forward Mounted Twin Light Blaster Cannons (Fire Arc Forward; Damage 4; Critical 4; Range [Close]; Linked 1).

One Port and One Starboard Turret Mounted Twin Light Suppression Cannons—these weapons' entire profiles use personal scale, not planetary scale. (Fire Arc All; Damage 10; Critical NA; Range [Close]; Blast 5, Disorient 4, Linked 1, Stun Damage).

HUNCHBACK CONSTRUCTION STRIDER

The Hunchback is a lightweight utility walker designed for construction and civil engineering work. Similar to the Republic's AT-PT, the Hunchback is a bipedal walker with a sturdy, lightly armored, slab-sided rect-angular command pod perched atop a pair of powerful reverse-artic-ulated legs. That's where the similari-ties end, however. The Hunchback carries no offen-sive weapons. Instead, a pair of articulated utility arms are mounted on each side of the cockpit. The arms carry a

wide array of tools such as plasma cutters, saws, welders, drills, compressed air guns, and small, dextrous manipulators for fine work. Two powerful floodlights flank the viewport, and the walker is equipped with a multi-spectrum sensor suite that contains a thermal imager, passive night vision, ultrasound transceivers, surface penetrating radar, and a number of other sophisticated sensors to assist an engineer in his work.

2	1	0	DEF: FORE/PORT/STARBOARD/AFT		ARMOR
SILHOUETTE	SPEED	HANDLING	0 - - 0		0
			HT THRESHOLD	SS THRESHOLD	
			7	6	

Vehicle Type/Model: Walker/All Terrain Construction Transport.
Manufacturer: Kuat Drive Yards.
Sensor Range: Close.
Crew: One pilot, one co-pilot/engineer.
Encumbrance Capacity: 12.
Passenger Capacity: None.
Price/Rarity: 28,000 credits/4.
Customization Hard Points: 3.
Weapons: One Forward Mounted Medium Tractor Beam Emitter (Fire Arc Forward; Damage –; Critical –; Range [Short]; Tractor 4).

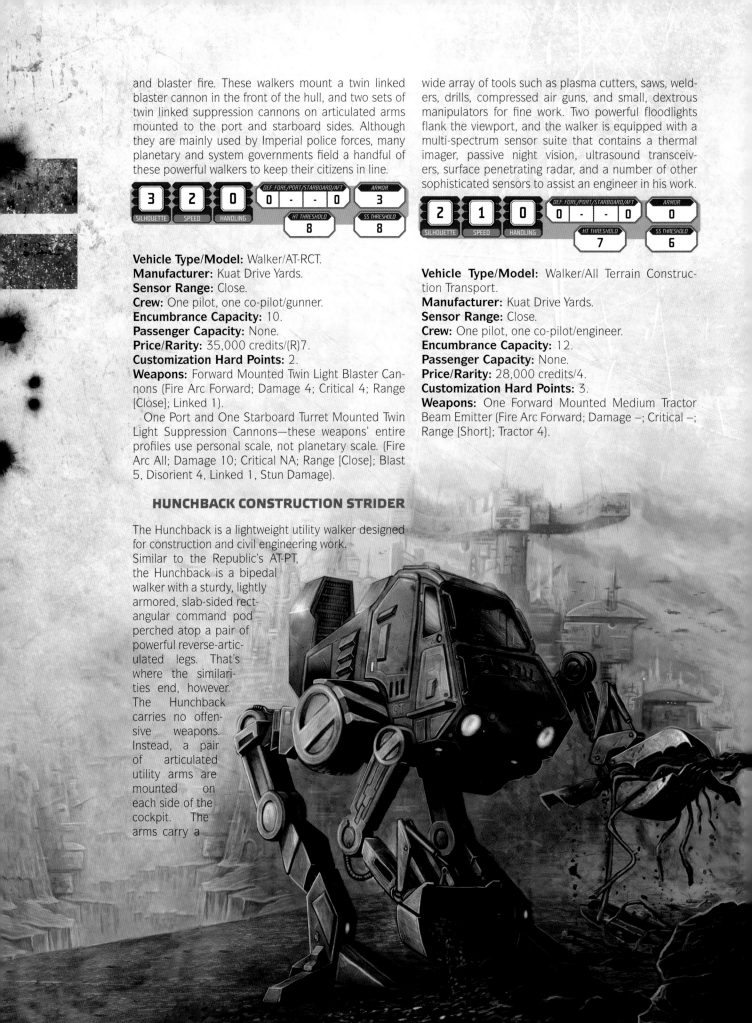

STARFIGHTERS AND PATROL BOATS

These small, quick vessels, typically loaded with powerful weapon systems and sensor suites, are perfect for the kind of skirmish and interdiction action typical in the Outer Rim.

YQ-400 MONITOR-CLASS SYSTEM PATROL SHIP

The Monitor-class system patrol ship is a droid operated vessel marketed to planetary and system governmental bodies for patrolling shipping lanes and hyperspace entry points. Roughly the size of a small freighter or large shuttlecraft, the YQ-400 is a curious looking vessel whose design shares little in common with other Corellian Engineering Corporation products. The vessel's largest hull section consists of a single, high-performance ion turbine that looks as if it would be more at home on an Imperial cruiser. This is shrouded in three thin, angular hull plates, one mounted dorsally and two mounted low on the port and starboard sides, that protect the power generators and secondary thrusters. It has a blunt, rounded bow section dominated by a single, massive, deep blue photoreceptor four meters across. This section houses the droid brain that runs the ship, as well as all of its communications, avionics, and sensor systems. While they are well armed with laser cannons and ion weaponry, and are no slouch in a fight, Monitor-class droid ships are programmed to never fire on another vessel unprovoked.

The droids that control the YQ-400s have a suspicious, officious personality and are possessed of near endless amounts of low cunning. Those individuals who work with them state that the droids are obsessive, worry about inconsequential details while often missing a larger picture, and have a tendency to speak and act like a peevish middle manager rather than a vigilant watcher. When in service, these vessels typically patrol a pre-determined route using only passive sensors to monitor space traffic, and are under orders to follow any suspicious vessel and report its whereabouts to system traffic control officers immediately.

These unique ships were conceived and built by the Nerfworks, a semi-secret projects laboratory jointly funded by both Corellian Engineering Corporation and the Loronar Corporation. Located at CEC-L Shipyard Lab 6671-x42, Nerfworks combines the shipbuilding expertise of CEC with the talented programmers and neural engineers of the Loronar Corporation. Largely ignored by higher ups of both companies and given free rein with company expense accounts, Nerfworks is tasked with making breakthroughs in droid/starship interfaces. However, it is unlikely CEC will back a major droid-controlled shipbuilding program in the near future.

MONITOR DROID PROFILE [RIVAL]

Skills: Cool 2, Gunnery 2, Piloting (Space) 3, Vigilance 2.
Talents: None.
Abilities: Multi-tasking Control (on its turn, the Monitor Droid may perform one Pilot-only maneuver and one Pilot-only action, then perform a number of additional actions needed to fire each of its functioning weapons once).

YQ-400 SHIP PROFILE

Hull Type/Model: Droid Operated Patrol Vessel/Monitor-class.
Manufacturer: The Nerfworks.
Hyperdrive: None.
Navicomputer: None.
Sensor Range: Long.
Ship's Complement: None, droid operated.
Encumbrance Capacity: None.
Passenger Capacity: None.
Consumables: Three Months.
Price/Rarity: 200,000 credits/8.
Customization Hard Points: 0.
Weapons: Dorsal Turret Mounted Twin Linked Medium Laser Cannon (Fire Arc All; Damage 6; Critical 3; Range [Close]; Linked 1).

Forward Mounted Twin Linked Heavy Ion Cannons (Fire Arc Forward; Damage 7; Critical 4; Range [Medium]; Ion, Linked 1, Slow-firing 1).

REGULATOR-CLASS PATROL VESSEL

Sienar Fleet Systems' Regulator-class patrol vessels have been a staple of intersystem law enforcement across the galaxy for decades. First introduced during the Clone Wars, the Regulator-class was designed as a high-performance pursuit craft and heavy interceptor with an eye toward policing and customs enforcement. Regulator-class ships are small for patrol boats, with an aggressively styled hull, oversized engines, and weapons systems slightly out of scale for such a small craft. Dedicated in-system craft, the short-legged Regulators have no hyperdrives and carry little in the way of provisions. Their interiors are incredibly cramped, with most of the space given over to the power, drive, flight, and weapon systems. Aside from the bare minimum facilities required to support their two man crew, Regulators also have a prisoner lockup that can hold up to six individuals in safety if not in comfort.

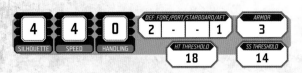

4	4	0	DEF: FORE/PORT/STARBOARD/AFT				ARMOR
SILHOUETTE	SPEED	HANDLING	2	-	-	1	3
			HT THRESHOLD			SS THRESHOLD	
			18			14	

Hull Type/Model: Patrol Boat/Regulator-class.
Manufacturer: Sienar Fleet Systems.
Hyperdrive: None.
Navicomputer: None.
Sensor Range: Medium.
Ship's Complement: One pilot, one co-pilot/engineer.
Encumbrance Capacity: 18.
Passenger Capacity: Six prisoners.
Consumables: Seven days.
Price/Rarity: 110,000 credits/6.
Customization Hard Points: 2.
Weapons: Forward Mounted Twin Linked Light Ion Cannons (Fire Arc Forward; Damage 5; Critical 4; Range [Close]; Ion, Linked 1)

Dorsal Turret Mounted Quad Laser Cannon (Fire Arc All; Damage 5; Critical 3; Range [Close]; Accurate, Linked 3).

FREIGHTERS AND TRANSPORTS

Pioneered by the great minds at Corellian Engineering Corporation, the ubiquitous modular light freighter was built for work in the Outer Rim territories. So common are freighters and transports in the Rim territories, shuttling colonists, laborers, tools, and machinery, that hardly anyone gives these hardy vessels a second look.

HT-2200 MEDIUM FREIGHTER

Corellian Engineering Corporation's HT-2200 is a lumbering, slab-sided medium freighter initially designed to capitalize on the success of CEC's wildly popular YT-series of light freighters. Solidly built and packed with state of the art avionics and cargo handling systems, these massive vessels are shaped like a tuning fork with the crew, weapons, and engineering sections in the central hull and four airtight cargo holds in the port and starboard booms. The trademark CEC conical cockpit is located amidships between the booms, giving the pilot and co-pilot a nearly 180 degree view of their surroundings. The ship's primary selling point, aside from its vast cargo capacity for a ship of its size, is the design of its holds. Each of the four holds is shielded, reinforced, and contains a number of modular cargo systems that allow them to be configured for different types of cargo. In addition, each hold has its own environmental systems, allowing the crew to adjust the temperature, atmospheric makeup, and gravity of each hold separately.

Initial reviews were favorable, and orders steadily came in from large shipping concerns in the mid and Outer Rim territories. As pilots and crews became

more familiar with them, however, they reported a number of serious shortcomings. While the hull and power distribution systems were designed to allow the types of modification and hot-rodding that CEC ships are famous for, the ships' primary power generator was woefully underpowered. In addition, thanks to these power shortcomings and the choice of Koensayr's single-tube ion drive as its primary drive, the HT-2200 proved slow and sluggish with poor acceleration and even poorer maneuverability. This, along with its surprisingly light weapons loadout, made the freighters easy pickings for pirates. Despite all of their inherent flaws, HT-2200s remain in limited production, thanks to their advanced cargo systems and sturdy hull.

5	2	-2	DEF: FORE/PORT/STARBOARD/AFT				ARMOR
SILHOUETTE	SPEED	HANDLING	1	1	1	0	5
			HT THRESHOLD			SS THRESHOLD	
			35			14	

Hull Type/Model: Freighter/HT-2200.
Manufacturer: Corellian Engineering Corporation.
Hyperdrive: Primary: Class 3, Backup: Class 15.
Navicomputer: Yes.
Sensor Range: Short.
Ship's Complement: One pilot, one co-pilot, one engineer, one loadmaster.
Encumbrance Capacity: 800.
Passenger Capacity: 8.
Consumables: Three months.
Price/Rarity: 140,000 credits/5.
Customization Hard Points: 5.
Weapons: One Dorsal and One Ventral Turret Mounted Medium Laser Cannon (Fire Arc All; Damage 6; Critical 3; Range [Close]).

HWK-290 LIGHT FREIGHTER

First designed decades before the Battle of Naboo, these tough little freighters were Corellian Engineering Corporation's first attempt to break into the rapidly expanding "executive light freighter" market. Unlike the relatively staid and workmanlike YT-series, which was marketed toward smaller profile traders and tramp freighter operators, the HWK-290 was targeted at wealthy, high-profile clients such as powerful interstellar shipping conglomerates and planetary governments. While they enjoyed modest success, and were highly praised for their performance and ease of operation, the Hawk-290s never reached the sales numbers of the more popular YT-series, and the entire line was discontinued during the Clone Wars to free up production lines for military use.

The Hawk-290 is a light, fast, agile craft designed for speed and comfort rather than heavy lifting. They are handsome vessels with lean, angular hulls and narrow, deeply tinted viewports that make them look fast and aggressive, even when parked in a hangar. While they were never designed to carry much cargo, the HWK-

series still
has a respect-
able lift capacity
for vessels of their size, and
are well suited for courier work and the
transportation of small, highly valuable cargoes. They
have light armor and were originally designed with no
weapon systems, relying instead on raw speed and
maneuverability for protection. Of course, being CEC
products, they are incredibly versatile and modular,
and most Hawks still plying the spacelanes are so
heavily modified as to be nearly unrecognizable.

SILHOUETTE	SPEED	HANDLING	DEF: FORE/PORT/STARBOARD/AFT				ARMOR
3	4	+1	1	-	-	1	2
			HT THRESHOLD		SS THRESHOLD		
			18		18		

Hull Type/Model: Freighter/HWK-290.
Manufacturer: Corellian Engineering Corporation.
Hyperdrive: Primary: Class 2, Backup: None.
Navicomputer: Yes.
Sensor Range: Short.
Ship's Complement: One pilot, one co-pilot.
Encumbrance Capacity: 75.
Passenger Capacity: 2.
Consumables: Three months.
Price/Rarity: 70,000 credits/7.
Customization Hard Points: 5.
Weapons: None.

YT-1200 LIGHT FREIGHTER

Built to replace Corellian Engineering Corporation's
revolutionary YT-1000 modular light freighter, the
YT-1200 was supposed to redefine the light freighter
concept. It featured the iconic saucer-shaped hull of
its predecessor, along with the trademark CEC modular design features and reliable ship systems. Improvements on the older ship's design
included an offset, side-mounted cockpit, more powerful engines, better sensors, and a more efficient cargo
handling system. Unfortunately, as is the case with
many sophomore efforts, the YT-1200 fell well short of
its predecessor in a number of important areas.

In a clear-cut case of trying too hard, CEC designers
set out not to build a well-built freighter, but to build
"the next YT-1000." They looked at market analysis
and customer feedback, identified what they believed
made the YT-1000 so successful, and designed the
new ship to simply do what the YT-1000 did in the
hopes of another wild success. Initial sales were very
good, but as customers became more familiar with
these new ships, complaints came pouring in. The
YT-1200 was seen as not enough of its own ship to
be really distinguished from the YT-1000. Customers
also reported the engines weren't powerful enough,
the internal systems were buggy, and the stock power
generators were prone to power surges and short cir-
cuits. Sales fell off sharply, and CEC eventually can-
celed production of the YT-1200 and retrofitted the
remaining stock with better systems, releasing those
refit ships as the YT-1210 and the YT-1250. Despite
their dismal commercial failure and lingering bad
reputations, the YT-1200 series freighters can still be
found on the used ship market.

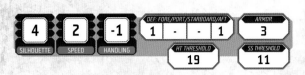

4	2	-1	DEF: FORE/PORT/STARBOARD/AFT				ARMOR
SILHOUETTE	SPEED	HANDLING	1	-	-	1	3
			HT THRESHOLD		SS THRESHOLD		
			19		11		

Hull Type/Model: Freighter/YT-1200.
Manufacturer: Corellian Engineering Corporation.
Hyperdrive: Primary: Class 3, Backup: Class 15.
Navicomputer: Yes.
Sensor Range: Medium.
Ship's Complement: One pilot, one co-pilot.
Encumbrance Capacity: 150.
Passenger Capacity: 6.
Consumables: Two months.
Price/Rarity: 90,000 credits/5.
Customization Hard Points: 5.
Weapons: One Ventral Turret Mounted Twin Light Laser Cannon (Fire Arc All; Damage 5; Critical 3; Range [Close]; Linked 1).

YT-1760 SMALL TRANSPORT

Released roughly thirty years before the Battle of Yavin, the YT-1760 is a small, fast, and agile light freighter in the vein of the older HWK-series. CEC's designers packed the new vessel with more powerful engines, upgraded maneuvering thrusters, and a sophisticated avionics package. Unfortunately, in their zeal, the 1760's designers went a little too far with their upgrades and produced a ship that, while fast and agile, was also high-maintenance, difficult to fly, fragile, and had a vastly reduced cargo capacity.

Never a company to let a few niggling problems hold them back, CEC put the YT-1760 into production despite its obvious shortcomings and poor focus testing. Initially, sales were quite robust. Its speed and small size attracted many small time shipping concerns and budget-minded planetary governments who used it as a courier, VIP shuttle, or for transporting small, delicate cargoes. Eventually, however, many owners discovered that the amount of time and money needed to keep the fragile little ship in space was more than the ship itself was worth, and sales dropped off dramatically. The introduction of the YT-1300 sounded the death knell for the 1760, and within five years, production of the 1760 was shut down.

4	4	+1	DEF: FORE/PORT/STARBOARD/AFT				ARMOR
SILHOUETTE	SPEED	HANDLING	1	-	-	0	1
			HT THRESHOLD		SS THRESHOLD		
			17		15		

Hull Type/Model: Small Transport/YT-1760.
Manufacturer: Corellian Engineering Corporation.
Hyperdrive: Primary: Class 1, Backup: Class 15.
Navicomputer: Yes.
Sensor Range: Short.
Ship's Complement: One pilot, one co-pilot.
Encumbrance Capacity: 70.
Passenger Capacity: 8.
Consumables: Two months.
Price/Rarity: 80,000 credits/5.
Customization Hard Points: 5.
Weapons: Dorsal Turret Mounted Light Laser Cannon (Fire Arc All; Damage 5; Critical 3; Range [Close]).

LUXURIOUS-CLASS YACHT

Relatively unknown and vastly under-appreciated, the *Luxurious*-class was Ghtroc Industries' only entry into the luxury yacht market. Smaller and faster than Soro-Suub's more popular Luxury 3000, the *Luxurious*-class ships were marketed toward aficionados of exclusivity and high performance. They possessed the singular, quirky charm common to Ghtroc products, and were, in their time, among the fastest and most finely appointed yachts in the galaxy. Each yacht was hand built from the keel up to the specifications of each owner. Ghtroc offered a dizzying array of options, allowing a buyer to hand pick everything from the ship's power systems to the fixtures in the captain's head. *Luxurious*-class yachts were especially popular among media moguls, professional ship racers, and sports stars. Even Raith Sienar himself owned one of these ships, a vessel rumored to be quicker than a TIE fighter and nearly indestructible.

Like other custom built starships, no two *Luxurious*-class are alike. That said, they do share a number of superficial similarities. Their hulls are relatively short and broad in the beam, and from above they resemble an oversized Y-wing starfighter. The forward half of the central hull is dominated by a half-domed, four decked, transparisteel fronted section that contains the command deck and bridge, staterooms, common area, and observation deck. Engineering and crew accommodations are located abaft the passenger decks in a spartan, utilitarian section, and the ship's powerful engines are housed in sleek port and starboard sponsons. While each ship has some of the best systems and accommodations to be found in a civilian vessel, they possess no combat capabilities and are relatively thin skinned.

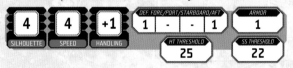

4	4	+1	DEF: FORE/PORT/STARBOARD/AFT				ARMOR
SILHOUETTE	SPEED	HANDLING	1	-	-	1	1
			HT THRESHOLD		SS THRESHOLD		
			25		22		

Hull Type/Model: Yacht/*Luxurious*-class.
Manufacturer: Ghtroc Industries.
Hyperdrive: Primary: Class 2, Backup: Class 12.
Navicomputer: Yes.
Sensor Range: Short.
Ship's Complement: One pilot, one co-pilot/engineer, one steward.
Encumbrance Capacity: 80.
Passenger Capacity: 12.
Consumables: Six Months.
Price/Rarity: 210,000 credits/6.
Customization Hard Points: 4.
Weapons: None.

CAPITAL SHIPS

Many ships big enough to be considered capital ships operating in the Outer Rim are not military vessels, but cruise liners, industrial ships, or scientific vessels.

ARMOS MODULAR TRANSPORT

The Armos Modular Transport has made inroads in the Outer Rim transport market due to its wide array of customization options. Their blunt, wedged-shaped hulls stretch aft to connect to a vertical trio of powerful engines. The keels taper to a point, while expanding outwards on higher decks to provide room for cargo and passengers. SoroSuub designed each deck to be modular, allowing the ship's crew to retrofit it to transport cargo, move passengers, serve as a tanker vessel, or even carry livestock. In addition, Soro-Suub equipped the Armos with reasonably powerful engines, a decent hyperdrive, and potent multi-band scanners. Combined with the modular layout, the company provided clients with a ship that can be retrofitted for almost any need.

SILHOUETTE	SPEED	HANDLING	DEF: FORE/PORT/STARBOARD/AFT				ARMOR
6	2	-2	2	1	1	1	4
			HT THRESHOLD		SS THRESHOLD		
			65		45		

Hull Type/Model: Transport/Armos.
Manufacturer: SoroSuub.
Hyperdrive: Primary: Class 2, Backup: Class 15.
Navicomputer: Yes.
Sensor Range: Extreme.
Ship's Complement: 150 officers and crew.
Encumbrance Capacity: 10,000.
Passenger Capacity: 1,000 (without cargo).
Consumables: Four months.
Price/Rarity: 780,000 credits/8.
Customization Hard Points: 4.
Weapons: None.

INDULGENT-CLASS LUXURY STARLINER

Some of the largest, most exclusive, most flamboyantly luxurious luxury liners in production, the ships of Leonore Luxury Liners Incorporated's *Indulgent*-class are spacegoing monuments to wealth and flagrant excess. Huge, slow-moving vessels the size of a heavy cruiser, these liners set the standard for luxury accommodations. Designed to provide the ultimate space travel experience, no expense was spared in their building and fitting out, and each ship is brimming with rare and exotic materials, all tailored to exceed each passenger's requirements. The *Indulgent*-class vessels are a limited production run sold exclusively to large cruise lines. They are a common sight in the more well traveled Outer Rim spacelanes, where they cruise a number of scenic areas and stop in the more civilized ports for resupply and a little slumming shore leave for passengers and crew. While they are susceptible to attack, these ships are not completely helpless. They mount sophisticated electronic countermeasures and a number of weapons to deal with all but the most persistent pirates.

SILHOUETTE	SPEED	HANDLING	DEF: FORE/PORT/STARBOARD/AFT				ARMOR
7	1	-1	2	1	1	2	2
			HT THRESHOLD		SS THRESHOLD		
			85		40		

Hull Type/Model: Starliner/*Indulgent*-class.
Manufacturer: Leonore Luxury Liners Incorporated.
Hyperdrive: Primary: Class 3, Backup: Class 12.
Navicomputer: Yes.
Sensor Range: Long.
Ship's Complement: 850 officers and crew.
Encumbrance Capacity: 3,200.
Passenger Capacity: 1,500 passengers.
Consumables: Six months.
Price/Rarity: 25,500,000 credits/7.
Customization Hard Points: 1
Weapons: Two Dorsal and Two Ventral Turret Mounted Twin Heavy Ion Cannons (Fire Arc All; Damage 7; Critical 4; Range [Medium]; Ion, Linked 1, Slow-Firing 1).

III

NEW HORIZONS AWAIT

"Out here, if a man tells you he got rich from a whole lot of hard work, you ask him 'Whose?'"

–Aver Lane, Kelsh Miner

The Colonist career covers a wide range of leaders and scholars. Colonists are found throughout the political spectrum. They fill the halls of learning. They heal the sick and wounded. They do business on both sides of the law, as conniving con men and dedicated law enforcement officers. Many Colonists perform for a living, whether they are entertaining professionally or putting on a show to further their own goals in public or private life.

Colonists might actually be pioneers and settlers of remote worlds. However, most are simply trying to make their way in the galaxy, sometimes for their own personal goals and desires and other times for the good of society as a whole. Most Colonists are dedicated to their own personal cause, for better or for worse, for themselves, their companions, and galactic civilization.

This chapter focuses on the adventures of Colonist characters. It discusses integrating the different types of Colonist characters into the adventuring party and gives advice for creating and adapting adventures and campaigns especially for Colonists.

This chapter also focuses on specific elements of the game that Colonists thrive on, and discusses how to make social encounters fun and interesting. It includes recommendations on how to use important bits of information in combination with skill check results. Specific encounter ideas, adventure suggestions, and campaign starters are also included. These Colonist-centric storylines are engaging to a variety of careers, but give the Colonist the opportunity to lead the way.

Rounding out the chapter are recommendations for granting Colonists XP and other rewards, as well as a discussion on combining the Colonist with other careers. It provides specific advice on granting XP for activities Colonists may perform on their adventures. Players can also find useful tips for fine-tuning their characters by combining the Colonist with specializations from other careers, creating variations on the themes already provided in this book and the **EDGE OF THE EMPIRE** Core Rulebook.

INTEGRATING COLONIST CHARACTERS

Colonist characters in **EDGE OF THE EMPIRE** embody a variety of social and supporting roles. This isn't to say that Colonists are solely supporting characters when the blaster fire begins, but that their standout skills are often away from the battlefield. In fact, it is the Colonist character that can often diffuse a deteriorating situation to prevent fighting from occurring in the first place. Of course, other Colonist characters are adept at cleaning up the mess, such as Doctors.

Integrating Colonist characters into the adventuring group is simple when they fall into a natural role that is commonly needed. Healers and leaders from most any background can find a place in the adventuring party. More difficult to explain can be the presence of a Scholar, Performer, or even the Marshal specialization. However, adventuring parties with a diverse makeup or mismatched characters can make for great adventures and inspire creative backgrounds to explain the characters' association with one another. This section discusses Colonists from a social and story idea basis. The **Dealing with Specialized Roles** section on page 65 addresses each specialization in detail.

WHY ARE THEY HERE?

Colonists are perhaps the career least likely to naturally fall into an adventuring lifestyle. With a couple of notable exceptions, most Colonists are more suited to professional pursuits, rather than hopping planets throughout the galaxy on a battered starship with a questionable crew. In addition, Colonists as a group tend to have higher social standing than many other careers. With this in mind, the Colonist player should develop a backstory that addresses how he arrived in his current situation. If he once held a higher office or position, what happened to it? If he was always at this social level, how does he fit in? What role does he fill, and how did he get into his current situation? See the **Professional vs. Adventurer** section on the opposite page for a closer look at specific Colonist specializations and their possible backgrounds.

See **Colonist Backgrounds** on page 10 for more universal backstories that can apply to most any Colonist specialization, or even non-Colonist careers. The GM can encourage the players to use some of these backgrounds to help give their party a common point of reference or use them to establish a related goal. The GM can also look to these backgrounds for inspiration when creating important or even just common NPCs. Some backgrounds, like the Baron, naturally involve characters far beyond a single PC or NPC.

LIFE AT THIS SOCIAL LEVEL

If the Colonist is living at a different social level than he is used to, the player should consider how the character views the change. Does he feel lucky simply to have survived his downfall or rapid ascendency? Is he depressed over the loss of reputation, wealth, power, or family? Does he feel vastly superior or inferior to his new companions, and is that attitude apparent in his words and deeds? Is he driven to return to his former station, content to have grown beyond it, or relieved to have avoided a worse situation?

Does the character still interact with those he knew in his former level of society? If so, how do they react to the character? Do they shun him, belittle him, or take pity on him? If the character rose to a higher level in society, are they jealous of his success?

The Game Master should use these feelings and interactions as a building block for his campaign. They give the GM the opportunity to engage the Player Character at a level fundamental to his character's background. It can and should influence the interaction between the Player Character and the Non-Player Characters.

Changes in social level are great story drivers that could interact with a character's Motivation and Obligation. Ascending characters might owe somebody a favor for promoting them to the position. Almost any Colonist might be the target of blackmail, and escaping it or rooting it out might be the source of his adventuring motivations. On the other hand, even

UP AND DOWN THE SOCIAL LADDER

The following table provides the player and Game Master with possible reasons for a Colonist's change in social position.

TABLE 3-1: SOCIAL POSITION CHANGES

Ascending	Descending
Heroic action.	Accused of being a Rebel agent or operative.
Imperial gratitude or earning favor.	Accused of being a Rebel sympathizer.
Important publication.	Convicted or accused criminal.
Political popularity.	Damaged reputation.
Public recognition.	Infamous scandal.
Successful business or performance.	Loss of wealth.
Sudden windfall.	Being fired from a job.

the most successful or popular public figure can be knocked down to the lowest levels of society by an addiction. See the **Up and Down the Social Ladder** sidebar on the previous page for additional ideas.

PROFESSIONAL VS. ADVENTURER

The life of a professional means a life of some stature, reputation, and economic benefit. When such characters become adventurers, they may or may not carry some or all of that previous life with them. Just because a Colonist is involved in an adventure or campaign, it doesn't mean he has left his past life completely behind. This section looks at each specialization and the interaction between the professional and the adventurer.

Of course, not all Colonists hold formal training or education, nor is it always necessary to do so. However, some specialized fields, such as doctors and medical personnel, should have some form of training in their background to justify their knowledge and abilities. There are far more natural leaders and performers than self-taught healers or researchers.

Most Colonist character backgrounds benefit from the player and GM thinking about and answering the following questions:

- Who is the character's most recent employer? Does the character still work for him? If not, why?

- What position does or did the character hold? What are the character's responsibilities?

- How much tolerance does the character's employer have to disruptions caused by the character's activities?

DOCTOR: IS THERE A DOCTOR IN THE HOUSE?

Doctors, medics, and other medical practitioners typically need years of training and experience in highly formalized settings to become competent in their field. However, not every Colonist Doctor needs to actually be medically trained. A character might be better suited to be a combat medic, emergency response medic, nurse, nurse practitioner, or any other profession along the scale of medical knowledge and practice. Given that most Player Characters start at a low level of competency, it is quite likely that their ultimate focus is determined by how long their adventuring career is, and what they pursue along the way.

Player Characters who wish for their adventuring career to be a sideline from their main medical profession need to come up with story ideas to balance the two. In the right adventure, perhaps the doctor is considered to be on a sabbatical or carrying out charitable works. This works well with rescue or missionary style adventures. The idea is that the doctor returns to normal duty for long stretches at a time. Campaigns with a lot of story-related downtime can easily accommodate this kind of storyline.

COLONISTS AND THE FORCE

Force using Colonists face the same challenges and difficulties as any other Force user, in that there is no easy way to train their abilities in the era of the Empire. Colonists may prefer nonviolent uses of the Force. Healing powers would be most easily concealed by medical personnel, while negotiators and other individuals who bargain and discuss political or economic deals find powers that influence their oppositions' minds particularly useful. Of course, how far the Colonist uses such a power greatly depends on their own moral code and their immediate situation.

If much of the Colonist's Force use is outside of combat, dark side transgressions might be more nuanced. Likewise, the character might suffer fewer obvious temptations in regards to the dark side than those who rely on it in combat. As very few, if any, opportunities exist to formally train their abilities, these characters are left to their own devices to determine right from wrong. The character should be rewarded for making the right decision through story advancement. Making the wrong decision might lead them down the path of the dark side, and the GM should take advantage of the opportunity to introduce more drama to the character's ongoing storyline.

Alternatively, not all doctors are as ethical as one would hope. The PC might currently be running a scam, might be running from a con gone wrong, or might even be trying to reform himself after a run-in with the law or after irritating the wrong underworld figure.

ENTREPRENEUR: PROJECT CONNECTIONS

Entrepreneurs come from virtually any walk of life. They are the least likely to need extensive training in their field, and the most likely to be self-starters able to learn on the job. They make connections through their business contacts that can be utilized in many adventures or campaigns. Entrepreneurs also have talents that enable them to receive regular credits and payments thanks to past ventures. The player should give thought to where that money comes from and why the character receives it.

Becoming involved in an adventure is less of an issue for the Entrepreneur than for other professions. The adventure itself might be part of the Entrepreneur's most recent business. The entire party might be working for or with the Entrepreneur on his grand scheme. The Entrepreneur might also be looking for the next big thing to invest in or start, looking for partners or areas in need of a particular service. The effects of past successes or failures tend to follow or catch up with the Entrepreneur over time.

MARSHAL: ALWAYS ON THE JOB

Marshal characters usually have a present or past interest in keeping the peace and protecting the public from the scum of the galaxy. In civilized areas, they receive intense training ranging from tactics to public relations to interrogations. In wilder regions of the galaxy, they might receive much less training and more on-the-job experience. There are few true self-made law enforcers, and those that try often end up as vigilantes or private investigators. Law enforcement is as much attitude as it is position. Marshal characters might be strictly by-the-book, following laws to the letter, or they might take a broader view, seeking their own version of justice that may not always align with every local law.

Adventuring Marshals must first decide if they are still currently employed as law enforcement officers, or if they are operating on their own. If they are still employed, they'll need to consider factors such as jurisdiction when moving about the galaxy. Generally, a Marshal's jurisdiction is limited to a specific location. This may be a sector, a sub-sector, a planet, or even a continent or city. What this location is can be determined by the player and GM at character creation, based on the character concept. However, it is almost never galaxy-wide. The only galactic governing body is the Empire, and it enforces its laws through its own powerful military forces.

One thing players and GMs should keep in mind, however, is the issue of reciprocity. While a law enforcement official may not be able to officially operate outside his jurisdiction, many local governments happily offer him a certain amount of latitude and flexibility when he operates in their territory. Provided the Marshal respects local laws, informs local law enforcement about who he's going after, and avoids causing too much of a mess, many local governments see aiding outside law enforcement as a cheap and easy way to get rid of undesirables. On the other hand, however, a Marshal may run afoul of the pride and egos of local law enforcement, who may take umbrage in someone else trying to do their job for them. In the end, how a certain locality reacts to jurisdictional and reciprocity issues is up the Game Master.

A Marshal's adventuring should be tied into his position and investigations. Undercover work often ties well into adventuring. However, the character is still subject to orders from above, and should sometimes receive assignments to new cases. Generally, the Marshal's investigations should either be tied into the ongoing story (maybe he's working to arrest one of the group's criminal adversaries), or should be something he can investigate as part of a side mission.

One alternative is for the Marshal to operate undercover, so that the party doesn't know his true position. He might even be investigating the party. This sort of story can be exciting and dramatic, but obviously puts the Marshal at odds with some or all of the other PCs. The GM should try to determine whether the players would like that gaming experience before proceeding.

PERFORMER: ALL THE UNIVERSE IS A STAGE

No matter their style of entertainment, Performers need an audience. Typically, Performers work individual projects, lasting days, weeks, or months. As the work ebbs and flows, Performers often relocate to take on a new project and find new opportunities. A Performer with a current job might be reluctant or unable to take part in a typical adventure at a moment's notice. On the other hand, Performers who live and work as part of a traveling show or some other kind of roving entertainment might find it easier to accommodate an adventuring lifestyle. Prosperous colonies may be willing to pay well for a rare opportunity to see live entertainment, whereas desperate colonies may still be willing to chip in some money just as a change of pace.

PC Performers may be seeking their next opportunity when falling in with the other characters. They might also hire their companions to help run a traveling show. In fact, the entire group could be a band or show, with other careers such as the Smuggler providing transport (and possibly trick shooting), an athletic Assassin using his agile grace in dance routines, or a Technician making music on his own, custom designed instrument. In this case, the Performer may be the lead singer or dancer for the group. Performers soon find new uses for their natural ability and performance skills when taking up the life of the typical EDGE OF THE EMPIRE adventuring party. Acting, in particular, is a useful skill to get the character and the party out of all kinds of difficult and inconvenient situations. That's not to say that Performers are always lying, but that a performance emphasizing or exaggerating the current situation can speed things along.

In addition, Performers often work with people from throughout the galaxy. As a production is staged, it includes anywhere from a few beings to hundreds or thousands of individuals to pull it off. Therefore, the Performer often runs into a familiar face or name when traveling the galaxy, especially in popular venues of the Performer's area of expertise. Such connections are always useful to the GM for sources of information, help, and credits. However, personalities and personal rivalries might also come into play, adding drama and intensity to an otherwise mundane exchange of information.

POLITICO: A LEADER IN ANY ARENA

The Politico character often finds it easier to adapt to his new situation than others of the Colonist career. As leaders, Politicos naturally gravitate toward trying to control or manipulate the situation. They have all the skills and expertise needed to step forward and take charge in any situation; although whether or not they

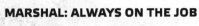

can actually use these skills properly depends on the Politico in question. Some may learn on the job, while others make rookie mistakes or unrecoverable gaffes, putting their companions in danger. Of course, some are able to talk their way out of their own messes, furthering whatever cause they have fallen into.

Adventuring Politicos come from a variety of government, corporate, and social backgrounds. They might be former government officials or employees that were fired, removed, quit, or failed to win elected positions. Though they might have made a few enemies, they're less likely than some to have old enemies pursuing them. Depending on their former post, they might have extensive connections to other individuals in similar roles in their region of operations.

It is uncommon for Politicos to continue their professional career while adventuring. While a few might be able to represent specific governments or companies for a short time when the adventure is compatible with their goals, Politicos soon find that the political difficulties generated by many adventures can overwhelm their career. However, a few Politicos might be able to sustain such a path by working for a non-government organization that has goals requiring a semi-independent operative.

SCHOLAR: EDUCATION NEVER ENDS

By his nature, the Scholar pursues education and knowledge. Research can take a great many forms, and not all of them require a purely intellectual pursuit. Schools, governments, corporations, and think tanks all commission very specific forms of study. The Scholar character might officially be attached to such an institution, but be allowed to research his effort on his own terms. Eventually, he must produce a report or conclusion to his research, which might be difficult to achieve when he is in the midst of other adventures.

Adventuring Scholars might be attached to a group due to professional needs or simple curiosity, or, as is often the case in **EDGE OF THE EMPIRE**, they might be on the run. Their previous positions may have turned intolerable because the character was banned or otherwise disallowed by an institution of learning. They may have inadvertently angered Imperial officials, backed Rebel sympathizers, or made an unrecoverable social or internal political gaffe. The Scholar may have even chosen the group as the focus of their research project, which could lead to some interesting and even hilarious party interactions. Scholars provide an adventuring group with unusual forms of knowledge and information that can provide new avenues of action. However, most Scholars are probably not a great source of interstellar connections outside of their specific areas of study.

DEALING WITH SPECIALIZED ROLES

Creating exciting and interesting encounters for Colonists can be more challenging for GMs than straightforward action or combat encounters. This section looks at encounters suitable for each specialization, and ways to reward characters for their skill and talent choices. Each entry in this section looks at general ways to focus encounters or parts of encounters on the Colonist, then provides a specific example illustrating one or more of those elements. The **Making Social Encounters Interesting** section on page 72 focuses on creating good social encounters, so that subject is only lightly touched on in this section.

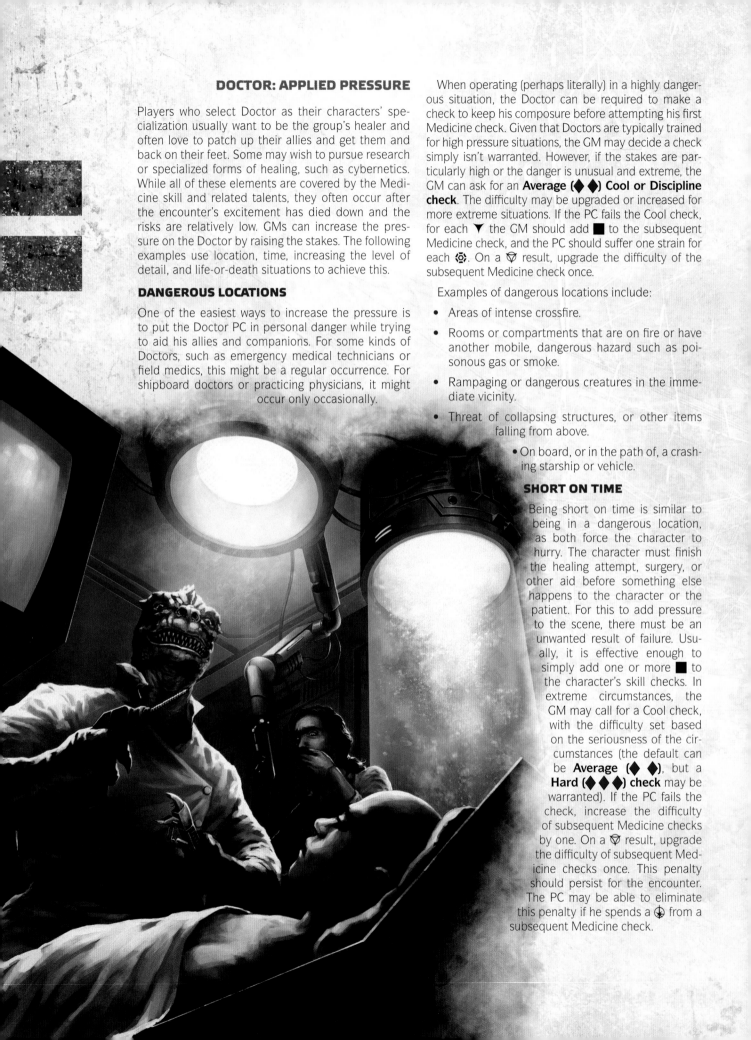

DOCTOR: APPLIED PRESSURE

Players who select Doctor as their characters' specialization usually want to be the group's healer and often love to patch up their allies and get them and back on their feet. Some may wish to pursue research or specialized forms of healing, such as cybernetics. While all of these elements are covered by the Medicine skill and related talents, they often occur after the encounter's excitement has died down and the risks are relatively low. GMs can increase the pressure on the Doctor by raising the stakes. The following examples use location, time, increasing the level of detail, and life-or-death situations to achieve this.

DANGEROUS LOCATIONS

One of the easiest ways to increase the pressure is to put the Doctor PC in personal danger while trying to aid his allies and companions. For some kinds of Doctors, such as emergency medical technicians or field medics, this might be a regular occurrence. For shipboard doctors or practicing physicians, it might occur only occasionally.

When operating (perhaps literally) in a highly dangerous situation, the Doctor can be required to make a check to keep his composure before attempting his first Medicine check. Given that Doctors are typically trained for high pressure situations, the GM may decide a check simply isn't warranted. However, if the stakes are particularly high or the danger is unusual and extreme, the GM can ask for an **Average (♦ ♦) Cool or Discipline check**. The difficulty may be upgraded or increased for more extreme situations. If the PC fails the Cool check, for each ▼ the GM should add ■ to the subsequent Medicine check, and the PC should suffer one strain for each ✪. On a ▽ result, upgrade the difficulty of the subsequent Medicine check once.

Examples of dangerous locations include:

- Areas of intense crossfire.

- Rooms or compartments that are on fire or have another mobile, dangerous hazard such as poisonous gas or smoke.

- Rampaging or dangerous creatures in the immediate vicinity.

- Threat of collapsing structures, or other items falling from above.

- On board, or in the path of, a crashing starship or vehicle.

SHORT ON TIME

Being short on time is similar to being in a dangerous location, as both force the character to hurry. The character must finish the healing attempt, surgery, or other aid before something else happens to the character or the patient. For this to add pressure to the scene, there must be an unwanted result of failure. Usually, it is effective enough to simply add one or more ■ to the character's skill checks. In extreme circumstances, the GM may call for a Cool check, with the difficulty set based on the seriousness of the circumstances (the default can be **Average (♦ ♦)**, but a **Hard (♦ ♦ ♦) check** may be warranted). If the PC fails the check, increase the difficulty of subsequent Medicine checks by one. On a ▽ result, upgrade the difficulty of subsequent Medicine checks once. This penalty should persist for the encounter. The PC may be able to eliminate this penalty if he spends a ⊕ from a subsequent Medicine check.

OUTSIDE INCOME

Holding a position outside of the adventuring group normally provides a source of income for the Player Character. While much of this extra income could be consumed by the character's everyday needs, such as rent and other services on his world of employment, easy credits can derail deliberately credit-starved campaigns without some planning.

Before play begins, the player and GM should discuss how the outside income might work with the campaign. Additionally, the GM should review the Entrepreneur talents and try to avoid granting characters of other Careers any benefits through story means that would diminish the Entrepreneur character's advantages and talent choices. Of course, another thing to consider is that the Entrepreneur character can take on outside work in addition to his Sound Investments talents; thus gaining the added benefits of his XP investment while still allowing all of the PCs to earn an income.

Income is usually deposited directly into the character's bank account. While such accounts are typically available in civilized space, there are plenty of places on any world or in any system that don't have access. Income is typically a set amount of credits that are deposited at consistent and predictable times.

Beyond the credits themselves, the characters must also be concerned with making it back to work on time, or otherwise maintaining their professional career. EDGE OF THE EMPIRE storylines typically deal with unsavory characters and situations that, if made public, might be looked down upon by employers, administrators, and possibly the public. The GM should consider what might happen if stories about the Player Character's exploits get back to his employer. Would he be fired or reprimanded? If the character comes from a highly civilized planet, is there a board of ethics or similar organization that could call the character in to justify his actions? These threats to the character's livelihood make good opportunities for new adventures. Long absences or surprise disruptions to the character's normal work schedule should negatively impact him, from a reduction in pay to a loss of a job.

EMERGENCY TRIAGE

Nothing adds to the pressure of treating the wounded like having multiple critically injured patients to diagnose and treat at the same time. The adventuring party might sustain multiple Critical Injuries as part of a vehicle or ship crash, combat, or industrial accident. The PCs might need to treat multiple NPCs for similar reasons. When treating two or more patients with Critical Injuries, the Doctor may make a **Daunting (◆◆◆◆) Medicine check** to assess a number of patients equal to his rank in the Medicine skill in a single round. The results of the check have the following effects:

- For each ✪, the Doctor adds ☐ to one Medicine check made to one patient.

- If the check fails, the Doctor adds ■ to his next Medicine check.

- Each ◉ immediately inflicts one strain on one patient, and each ✪ immediately heals one strain on one patient, representing the Doctor's minimal treatment during the assessment process.

- On a ▽ result, one patient selected by the GM must make a **Hard (◆◆◆) Resistance check** or suffer one Critical Injury. ◉ and ✪ are ignored for the Resistance check.

- On a ✦, the Doctor may upgrade the ability of all of his subsequent Medicine checks once during the encounter, or may immediately heal one Critical Injury on one patient.

INCREASING THE LEVEL OF DETAIL

In this instance, performing a Medicine check becomes the heart of a major encounter for the Doctor. Instead of making a single Medicine check to heal an important character, the Doctor might need to make several for different stages of an operation or extended treatment. To increase the engagement of this kind of encounter, the GM should give the Doctor a variety of treatment options, using the outcome of the skill check to lead to the next option. The options should have an obvious risk versus reward element to them, usually pitting speed of treatment or healing time against safety.

To account for leaps of logic or aid from sources beyond medical skill and practice, the GM may have the PC make Knowledge skill checks. For example, when treating a species unfamiliar, or at least less familiar, to the Doctor, the PC might make a Knowledge (Xenology) check for insight into the proper treatment. Success might upgrade the ability of the Doctor's Medicine skill for one roll, whereas failure might upgrade the difficulty of the roll. ✪ or ◉ might add ☐ or ■, respectively. A successful check might also allow the Doctor to attempt to heal one Critical Injury and one wound for each ✪. Knowledge (Education) and Knowledge (Lore) are also useful skills in some situations. Occasionally, even Knowledge (Core Worlds) and Knowledge (Outer Rim) may add insight.

ENTREPRENEUR: CASHING IN

The Entrepreneur specialization features a combination of toughness, the ability to bounce back from psychological stress and strain, access to funds, and unique ways to spend them. The Entrepreneur is typically no combat expert, but greatly aids the party in many other areas of need. With a regular source of income combined with ways to buy himself out of problem situations or buy critical information with ease, the Entrepreneur is a great enabler when the party needs help.

Encounters highlighting the Entrepreneur should feature opportunities to make use of his readily available source of credits—the Sound Investments talent. These include opportunities for negotiating deals, selling goods legally, and paying his way to social encounter success by spending his credits. Encounters that inflict strain on the character are countered by the Rapid Recovery talent.

CASHING OUT

Because the Sound Investments talent grants credits to the Entrepreneur in each game session (as opposed to each major chapter or adventure), the character may be entitled to credits at unusual times of the narrative. In many cases, this isn't an issue. The credits simply arrive in the character's bank account while he is off adventuring, and he can access the credits via a specialized account. However, when the character is in an isolated location, both the player and the GM might need to come up with creative ways for the character to receive the credits, or some sort of equivalent value. Tapping into the character's backstory or current events are great ways to better engage the character in the story. There are occasions where the PC simply isn't able to receive the funds, so the GM should note those times and be prepared to grant the credits when the PC's situation changes. The credits accumulate for use in future sessions.

WHEELING AND DEALING

Thanks to the career and bonus career skills, the Entrepreneur is likely to be the negotiator in the party, with secondary support in Knowledge skills. With the Entrepreneur front and center, it enables him to use his social skills to creatively deal with allies and enemies alike. GMs can prepare by thinking about the NPCs' approach to negotiation, and making some notes about their likely positions and how they respond to the PC's dealings and skill checks.

MARSHAL: EDGE OF THE LAW

The Marshal uses a combination of investigative talents and pure toughness to keep the peace and take down the bad guys. He fits a variety of overlapping roles—sometimes as a leader, other times as an investigator, and often as a combatant. He is able to operate on his own, which is often the case even in heavily populated regions of the galaxy.

Assuming that the Marshal character is still a law enforcement officer, private investigator, or works for a semi-official legal entity, the player probably expects to get an opportunity to investigate criminal activity and capture criminals at large. In some respects, the Marshal is similar to the Bounty Hunter when tracking down criminals on the run. The differences lie in the weight of the Marshal's legal authority (if any), access to allies in the legal profession, and a need to follow the law in carrying out his duties.

INVESTIGATOR

The Marshal is adept at many stages of investigation, thanks to the specialization's range of talents. The Marshal can increase physical and mental toughness, making him better able to soak up damage and shake off debilitating statuses compared to some other characters and Colonists. The Good Cop and Bad Cop talents help his allies question suspects or any other individual. The Marshal might also take enough talents to become a quick and deadly shot, setting him further apart from most Colonists.

Whether it is a true criminal investigation or simply a search for information commonly required in adventures, the GM should take the Marshal's abilities into account. Criminals and other targets of pursuit can inflict a fair amount of damage on the Marshal, and he's tough enough to take it. From a roleplaying standpoint, the GM should be prepared for the good cop/bad cop routine, and think about how the NPC responds under the pressure of questioning. When preparing an investigation, the GM needs to map it out and consider the following points:

- Establish exactly how the crime or event occurred.

- Determine what clues were left behind. Be prepared to carefully add clues if the PCs come up with ideas that might have logically occurred.

- Determine which PCs or NPCs have helpful information, and who is willing to share it (and why or why not).

- When the PCs use the good cop/bad cop routine during questioning, the GM should determine how the NPC reacts, and to whom. Some NPCs might cave immediately to a bad cop, while others tough it out, only to respond to the good cop. The GM should also prompt the PCs to discuss ahead of time which approach they think will succeed.

- Is there a cover up? If there is, who's behind it? Local law enforcement is an obvious choice, but corporate interests, government authorities, or even celebrities could be behind the cover up.

- Is the investigated crime one of many similar events, or is it one-time action?

- Who are the criminal's allies and how far would they go to help him?

- For an unexpected twist— are there Force users involved? A Force user might snarl a typical investigation by using a Force power to do something otherwise inexplicable. Given that Force users are very rare, it might take a while for the thought to occur to the investigator and the player, so the GM should shroud the truth in other possibilities that can be peeled away during the investigation.

- What are the consequences if the suspect is caught, killed, or escapes? These should be viewed as personal to the Marshal, and from a larger story standpoint. Will the suspect's allies seek revenge?

PERFORMER: ENTER STAGE LEFT

The Performer specialization offers a range of skills and talents that can be interpreted to build a variety of performer types. Using the Smooth Talker talent as an example (see page 31), an actor might select Charm to make the audience like him, while a stage magician might take Deception to help him misdirect the audience's attention. All Performers exemplify their ability to distract, captivate, or (in the case of a comedian or actor) even annoy individuals through Distracting Behavior. Physical performers like dancers, daredevils, or acrobats translate their abilities into faster recovery and second chances via Second Wind and Natural Athlete.

The Performer has among the most active talents of any specialization's talent tree, with very few passive talents available. This means that the Performer that invests in talents is always on a lookout to use them. The GM should note which talents the character has and prepare accordingly. For example, the player may have better skill check results due to Smooth Talker.

A WAY WITH WORDS

The Distracting Behavior talent can be one of the more disruptive combat-related talents, especially as the character takes on additional ranks of the talent and the Improved Distracting Behavior talent. Each additional rank expands its range, so while at first it only affects opponents engaged with the PC, it soon affects greater numbers at longer distances. While it applies only one or two ⬡ to the enemy's combat related checks against any target, it decreases the likelihood of the target activating Critical Hits through spending ⬡, or granting benefits to the target's allies in the form of ☐.

However, it is important to remember just how important this ability can be outside of combat, as well. Distracting Behavior affects all checks, not just combat checks. This could easily be a Performer telling an engaging story in the midst of negotiations (or flirting with the rival negotiator) to throw an opponent off and get them to agree to something without thinking about it. Likewise, a competent actor could play the role of a dangerous psychopath during an interrogation to rattle the suspect, allowing the interrogator to learn valuable information.

Over time, these tactics can have serious effects on the impact of NPCs. The GM can somewhat limit the talent's use by encouraging the PC to spend the maneuver on other activities—such as moving out of harm's way. Some creatures are immune to the effects—particularly those without intelligence. While language barriers are purposefully reduced in **EDGE OF THE EMPIRE**, there are individuals who won't understand the PC, and it may take extra time or effort to get the point across to them. The effect might also simply become less impactful when used time after time—the target gets used to the insults or PC actions and begins to ignore them. This might happen after only a few rounds.

PCs that suffer a lot of strain are also less likely to risk more loss using the talent. From a roleplaying viewpoint, the player should be encouraged to develop an array of insults that can be bantered about. If they become too repetitive, mood-breaking, or are simply not very good, the player can forego the description.

POLITICO: TALKING POINTS

The Politico lives and dies—sometimes literally—by his ability to talk his way out of trouble or manipulate a social situation to get his own way. Any encounter dominated by negotiation, investigation, or discussion is an opening for the Politico to influence events. Often, the player recognizes that his character likely has the best chance of succeeding from a game mechanics standpoint and naturally speaks up and takes the lead. Whether or not the Politico is an actual leader of the adventuring group is left up to the players and the story. However, the GM should look for opportunities for the Politico to play the leadership role, if only for a short time.

On the other hand, the Politico may not be the best choice for every situation. The GM should challenge the party by introducing NPCs that are either less keen on dealing with the character or naturally seek out other character types—such as a technician who needs to speak to another technically-minded person about very specific and important details. While the Politico might not take the lead, he can still offer advice and other avenues of discussion or negotiation.

RHETORICAL SET-UP

When a Politico character has selected the Inspiring Rhetoric and Improved Inspiring Rhetoric talents, the GM can set up encounters to give him opportunities to maximize these talents. First, the encounter must inflict strain on the Politico's allies. Ideally, much of this strain affects several PCs over the course of a round or two, and to the point that remaining conscious might be a real concern. The strain can also be quickly generated by suffering ⊛ on most any skill check. The PCs should also be suffering from a ■ or two. When the Politico uses Inspiring Rhetoric and Improved Inspiring Rhetoric simultaneously, it aids his allies on both counts by restoring strain and granting ☐.

For example, the PCs are battling a collection of Trandoshan thugs deep in a decrepit factory complex. The wind suddenly shifts, sending a waft of thick, brown poisonous gas across the area. The gas causes the PCs to make one or more Resilience checks. Those that fail suffer significant strain, and those that succeed still suffer a lesser amount. On top of that, the dense gas also inflicts a ■ or more to all ranged attacks, as well as on subsequent Resistance checks once a PC fails the check. Now when the Politico uses his Rhetoric related talents, the party gets a big boost.

THE ART OF BERATING THE ENEMY

The Politico talent Improved Scathing Tirade combined with a high Coercion skill can be particularly devastating to enemies within close proximity to the PC. ■ can really disrupt an enemy's chances of success, especially if inflicted over multiple rounds. This action is equally likely to take place during combat and affect combat skills as it is to take place during negotiation or other social interactions, possibly derailing the opponent in the process. However, while an angry NPC usually strikes back with an attack while in combat, circumstances change when used in other situations.

A PC unleashing a Scathing Tirade against an opponent naturally draws attention to both. If the Scathing Tirade occurs in a public place or delicate negotiation, there may be roleplaying consequences as others in the area respond to the disruption. The opponent may suddenly have friends step up to help, or draw the attention of good samaritans willing to break up any problems before they progress too far.

If a PC relies too heavily on Improved Scathing Tirade, certain tactics can help bring its use back under control. The GM can have opponents engage the PC to the point that the PC has other things he must use his action on, rather than this talent. Melee attacks can do this, but so can environmental hazards that force the PC to spend his actions to save his own life. Sometimes, the target is simply unimpressed or becomes disinterested and inured to the PC's shouting and taunts after a few rounds. This may be represented by upgrading the difficulty of subsequent checks, or eventually making the NPC immune.

SCHOLAR: INFORMATION FROM EVERYWHERE

Many adventures rely on information discovery as much as blasting away at enemies. The Scholar is adept at revealing key information in a short amount of time. A competent Scholar can accelerate the party's investigations and dig out difficult to find information from high class resources that may not otherwise be open to the PCs.

Scholars living on their own at the edges of society or the galaxy naturally take on different areas of expertise than their initial studies might have suggested. Some pick up leadership skills or use their information and knowledge as a major advantage in certain negotiations, deceptions, and other social situations. In fact, some isolated colonies or settlements might welcome the broad range of knowledge a Scholar brings, and even pay the individual well to figure out long standing problems or mysteries of their locale or social group.

AVENUES OF LEARNING

Scholars with the Respected Scholar talent (see page 67 of the **EDGE OF THE EMPIRE** Core Rulebook) decrease the difficulty of interacting with institutes of learning. The GM must be prepared for the Scholar character to seek out such organizations regularly when he is researching problems for the party. As these sorts of events are not commonly singled out in adventures, the GM must be flexible enough to make up something on the fly. Not every settlement or city has such a location, but every major city and world has one or more.

Each institute should have an evident institutional personality, even when the PC visits only for a short time. The institute also needs a difficulty level associated with it, which is applied to the PC's social skill checks when dealing with beings at the facility. To get the most out of the talent, the difficulty should be high enough for the talent's offset to be effective. PCs other than the Scholar should also need to

TABLE 3-2: INSTITUTIONAL DIFFICULTY LEVELS

Institution Type	Difficulty Level
Secondary education, local ad hoc research group	Easy (◆)
Low level university, low level think tank, startup research group	Average (◆ ◆)
Average university, mid level think tank, corporate research group	Hard (◆ ◆ ◆)
Elite university, high level think tank, top-level corporate research group	Daunting (◆ ◆ ◆ ◆)

engage the institute for story reasons and so that the Scholar's advantage becomes more evident. Some example institutions and difficulty settings are on **Tables 3–2: Institutional Difficulty Levels** and **3–3: Institutional Personality and Situation Modifiers**. The GM should use the type to find the base difficulty, then modify it based on the institutional personality and situation. While usually only one institutional personality should be used, they can be combined with one or more situational modifiers. Other factors may also come into play, such as the Scholar's reputation.

Once a Scholar has access to an institute of learning, he may be able to gain access to a variety of the organization's resources and departments. The Scholar may be able to persuade or otherwise manipulate the situation to gain the access he needs. Perhaps a teaching hospital or medical program might provide needed aid. Research labs might help solve a mystery or illness, or be manipulated to analyze or produce something the PCs need. Some schools may have a machine shop or advanced electronics lab. The Scholar can provide the party with a new source of resources through schools, universities, corporate labs, think tanks, and more.

DROID SUPPORT

One Scholar talent that players might overlook is Speaks Binary (see page 67 in the **EDGE OF THE EMPIRE** Core Rulebook). This talent grants a ■ per rank of Speaks Binary on checks to direct droids. While this might most naturally occur with research-related droids, there is no limitation on the type of droid under the Scholar's command. This gives the PC an advantage when working with most any droid, including droid pilots, gunners, and battle droids. For a party with a medical droid, the scholar's direction can be a nice boost on any healing check.

The GM should remember a few points about Speaks Binary. One, it only works on NPC character droids, not PCs. Two, while simply pointing to the droid and saying "do this thing for me" is technically enough to activate the talent, the GM should encourage the player to be specific and say something special about the direction to improve the roleplaying and creativity of the situation. Since Speaks Binary is passive and doesn't require an action, any such direction shouldn't interfere with the Scholar's normal actions in combat rounds.

TABLE 3-3: INSTITUTIONAL PERSONALITY AND SITUATION MODIFIERS

Institutional Personality	Situation Modifier
Arrogant	Upgrade difficulty twice
Egotistical	Add ■
Frightened	Add ■
Desperate	Add □
Grounded	Add □
Threatened	Upgrade difficulty once

MAKING SOCIAL ENCOUNTERS INTERESTING

Social encounters occur in virtually every **EDGE OF THE EMPIRE** game session. They are the basis for discovering new information as the player characters search for clues and ideas about their current mission or other pursuits. They are fantastic roleplaying opportunities that can add plenty of fun to a game session while providing memorable moments from an adventure or campaign.

However, without careful planning, poor Game Master responses can turn any conversational scene into a dull information dump. Most social encounters are handled on the fly, but major scenes benefit from planning. This minimizes pauses in the scene and breaks in the action, usually caused by the GM tries to work out the many facts the NPC characters might know while negotiating or discussing information with the PCs. This section explores ways to make social encounters more interesting for everyone. Some suggestions involve game mechanics, while others speak to the story and characters involved in a given scene.

USING TALENTS IN SOCIAL ENCOUNTERS

Most PC talents are designed and worded to be used in combat or structured play encounters. However, talents can also be used outside of combat, in social and other situations. This section provides additional guidance for using talents in non-combat situations, and how to adapt and translate the terms when the restrictions of the combat round are not in play.

USING TALENTS OUTSIDE COMBAT

When a player wants to use a talent in a non-combat context, the GM should first assess if it should work outside of combat. Combat-specific talents usually have no role outside of combat, just as talents that specify "after an encounter" are not to be used in the middle of an encounter. Other talents may fall into a gray area in which the talent could be used outside of combat, but doing so wouldn't provide any clear advantage. Talents that convert one type of action into another (such as a maneuver to an incidental action) are an example of these.

The GM should remember that an encounter is any specific set of events within a short time frame, not just combat. Talents that define actions or effects by encounter operate the same in a non-combat encounter as a combat encounter. When using a talent that is activated by a specific action—such as using a maneuver to perform the Intense Focus talent (see page 137 of the **EDGE OF THE EMPIRE** Core Rulebook)—the GM may limit the number of uses if the player is abusing the spirit of the talent. Talents that use maneuvers may be used once before each check, whereas talents that use actions might be used once per non-combat encounter.

DON'T FORGET THE SETBACK DICE!

Many talents grant a benefit that removes one or more □ from a skill check. However, since □ are not normally automatically included in the dice pool for a given check or task, it is up to the GM to add them in. GMs should develop a habit of regularly applying (or at least considering adding) □ to skill checks, so it does not become a game of applying a penalty simply to let the character take it away. While some checks automatically add □, this tends to happen less often in social encounters than it does in combat or piloting.

For example, in the case of Intense Focus, suffering one strain in exchange for upgrading the ability of a skill check might be used once on every check a PC makes, because he finds the loss of a few points of strain to be a minimal hindrance. In combat, giving up maneuvers or strain is riskier and more limiting to the character's actions than when outside of combat. Outside of combat, the GM might allow a reasonable number of uses, perhaps equal to the character's Intellect rank. Such limitations should only be required if a player is abusing the lack of limitations on a given talent.

TALENT TIMING IN SOCIAL ENCOUNTERS

Some talents impose time limits or award effects based on a certain amount of time during a combat round. Outside of combat, these talents function in a similar fashion, though they might not occur as rapidly as within the combat round. For example, the Distracting Behavior talent (see page 32) specifies that a number of enemies suffer ✪ until the beginning of the next turn on combat checks. If used outside of the combat round, the talent functions for as long as the character wishes to keep it active, or until the character starts using skills or activities that take more concentration or time to use effectively. Alternatively, the GM might rule that the talent affects the next check of up to three NPCs. The key is to find the balance between keeping the game fun but not abusing a rule or a GM's ruling.

EXCEEDING STRAIN THRESHOLDS IN SOCIAL ENCOUNTERS

Some talents cause the target or user to suffer strain, potentially sending him beyond his strain threshold. When in the midst of a social encounter, it may not make narrative sense for a character to pass out from exceeding his strain threshold. Instead, if a target exceeds his strain threshold, he is overwhelmed by the situation or is badgered into submission. He gives into his opponent's demands and is otherwise ineffective for the rest of the encounter.

When that happens, the affected character:

- Cannot perform actions, and can only perform basic maneuvers or incidentals such as moving or pulling out a cigarra and puffing on it angrily.

- Cannot aid others.

- Can talk and make his feelings known, but they are ineffective or ignored. This is primarily true when the character is a PC interacting with NPCs; although if groups want to roleplay their PCs being petulant, angry, or frustrated and the other PCs are ignoring him, that is perfectly acceptable.

- Can move around without affecting his opponent.

- Can use certain talents such as Hard Headed, with the GM's approval.

CONTROLLING THE FLOW OF INFORMATION

One key to encouraging interesting conversations in social encounters is the flow of information. Revealing key points, surprises, and offers at just the right time can make negotiation much more interesting. While the GM controls the way information is conveyed to the PCs, the PCs control the revelation of their own information and terms. In some ways, the GM can encourage the exchange of critical information for a scene by controlling what information is given and when. Published adventures usually cover this in broad strokes, giving specific opportunities for the PCs to learn specific points along the way. This section discusses how to fine-tune this approach for specific scenes and encounters. Of course, no amount of staging and encouragement can really predict how the PCs will carry out a discussion, and the characters will surprise the GM regularly. Adapting and adjusting on the fly is key, and part of the fun for the GM.

FEEDING THE PCS

During any negotiation or social encounter in which the Player Characters are attempting to advance the story and learn something new, they must have information to work with. The PCs may generate their side of the story completely on their own. The GM may also feed them information along the way. Usually, social encounters are a combination of the two.

In free-form games where the storyline is pushed along by the PCs more than a set plot generated by the GM or published adventure, it is up to the PCs to

create and relay any tidbits of information that they might find useful. The GM can guide the way a bit, with leading questions from the NPCs involved. The GM can also shake up the conversation with unexpected questions, accusatory statements, and genuine threats from the NPCs. Dropping unexpected bits of information or critical secrets into the discussion can ramp up the drama in a hurry.

In published or preplanned encounters, the GM has a set amount of information to dole out. Naturally, not every piece of information is always conveyed, particularly if the characters pursue a different line of questioning or discussion. The GM can sometimes bring the conversation back around to points he might wish to make, but it can be a challenge to do this in a casual, free-flowing fashion.

However, the information exchange may occur in ways beyond simple conversation. During the encounter, the GM may have characters make various Knowledge or other skill checks upon learning new details during the conversation. The GM might verbally tell the characters the results, which is fine if all of the characters logically could know or see the information for themselves. However, it is more likely that only one or a few characters might stumble on to an important realization during the encounter, and that they can't quickly tell

the others what they've learned. In these cases, the GM should write the information down as a note that can be passed around as needed.

As writing separate notes takes time away from the encounter and forces a pause in the game, the GM should consider writing a few notes ahead of time that can easily be picked up and passed out as needed. The GM can scribble a few minor changes if needed before handing notes out at the table. Notes should be short and to the point; typically a few sentences can convey the information. If the PC needs more details, he can either ask verbally or via a return note.

One advantage to using notes is that it enables the GM to tailor a specific response to the PC involved. It might include information of which the other PCs are unaware, making it more interesting for the PC with the note to decide whether he wants to reveal it. In **Edge of the Empire**, the diverse PC backgrounds often hold secrets and inconvenient topics that PCs may not want revealed to the party.

Tailoring notes and information has other advantages. If the GM

EXAMPLE OF PLAY

Below is a brief example of inserting new information into a scene during the course of an encounter. Sometimes the GM has the PC make a skill check. At other times the GM hands over the information if the PC should be able to work it out on his own, or simply to keep the scene moving and interesting. This example features the GM and four players. One of the players has a character named Herol, a Colonist with the Politico specialization.

GM: "You're taken before Sharune the Hutt. He's obviously angry and sneers upon seeing you. An armored human stands next to him. Sharune says, 'tell me why I shouldn't hand you over to this bounty hunter for the credits you owe me. Clearly you've angered someone else even more than me. Impressive, but also profitable for me, unless you have a better deal?'"

The GM has the PCs make a Knowledge (Underworld) check to recognize the bounty hunter. Herol succeeds well enough to gain a fair amount of information. The GM hands Herol's player a note with the bounty hunter's name, Kinn, as well as the fact that the hunter used to go by the alias Triar. Triar used to work against Sharune, and Herol already knows the circumstances from an earlier game session.

Herol: "Sharune, I can't believe you fell for this guy's con game. Don't you recognize our old friend Triar? Wonder what he did to your best lieutenant last year. Go ahead Triar, take off that mask and tell us where you took him."

GM: "The Hutt looks surprised, then signals his guards to move into position…"

releases the notes in a specific order, he can help guide the conversation. This essentially gives the player a heads-up as to the direction the encounter could go, with each revelation pushing the negotiation or the discussion in a particular direction. This can increase a scene's drama considerably.

INFORMATION TYPES

Here are presented some examples of bits of information that can be inserted into an ongoing discussion, illustrating ways that well-timed revelations might alter the conversation or push it in a certain direction. PCs might also learn or deduce some of this information through skill checks during the negotiation or conversation.

Though the information may be revealed in conversation, the GM should not overlook the opportunity to use non-verbal cues for added drama and subtlety. An NPC's words might say one thing, while his furrowed brow or reddening face imply something else. There are also opportunities for cross-species confusion or missed cultural cues that can add to a scene. A human with little experience dealing with a Gand might completely miss useful cues, while the human's better traveled companion might clue him in, or use the knowledge to take a more important role in the scene.

Anger Management: The PC notices that the opposing character's level of anger and frustration rises and falls depending on the subject matter and possibly who is talking during the conversation. The PC may be able to figure out what the character's trigger points are, and manipulate them to his advantage.

Blown Cover: Someone's real name or alias is suddenly revealed during the conversation. An NPC might call an ally by his real name instead of the one the

PCs know him by. For a more significant reveal, the NPC might reveal a PC's actual name to his unaware companions. However, the GM should maximize the drama with multiple consequences for the name's revelation, especially if the player (and PC) are hiding it for a good story reason.

Connection Revealed: Someone's family, business, or economic relationship is revealed or hinted at during the conversation. The PC might be able to use the connection as leverage.

Fraud Revealed: One of the parties makes a noticeable blunder when posing as a person in a position that he doesn't truly hold. Essentially, the individual makes a mistake that no person knowledgeable or experienced in a specific field or circumstance would ever make. The mistake may not be noticeable to all parties, just those with enough experience or background knowledge to realize it.

Love and Romance: The NPC might suddenly reveal love and affection toward a PC, which may be real or just a ploy to gain an advantage. Alternatively, the PC might realize that the character has a crush or is otherwise attracted to the PC or one of the PC's allies, then take advantage of it. Of course, there might be a genuine attraction between the two, which can quickly complicate the situation in unexpected ways.

Offer Terms: The NPC might give specific offers, and the players may not know if it is a good offer or not, but their character should. The GM should convey enough information about the positives and negatives of the offer that the character should know in order to give the player a chance to respond accordingly.

Technical Data: A character can make use of detailed knowledge of a piece of technical data, device, vehicle, or starship that is discussed during the encounter.

Unexpected/Unintended Insult: Either the PC or NPC accidentally or unknowingly insults the other party. The insult might come in the form of a slight against one of the negotiator's associates or an offhand comment that might not offend someone of the same political or cultural persuasion, but definitely insults one or more of the people involved in the conversation. Not every PC may pick up or be offended by the insult, causing a range of reactions across the characters.

BEWARE THE INFORMATION DUMP!

Given the nature of roleplaying games, there are often times when a PC should know much more about a given situation or subject than the player knows or could learn by playing out a scene. There is a natural temptation for the GM to simply explain the situation or describe the details for the character's use. Unfortunately, this can lead to long narratives that leave the characters with little to do other than listen. A better way is to divide up the information, so the characters can learn it from several sources, or refer to it over the course of the adventure. This allows them to learn the information closer to when they need it. Details that are described too far from their point of usage often get lost in a longer adventure or campaign.

USING DRAMA IN SOCIAL ENCOUNTERS

While any encounter might include drama, specifically designing an encounter to be dramatic without resorting to combat or violence can take some work. While a dramatic social encounter certainly could lead to fighting, and often does, there is plenty of excitement to be had without blaster fire and lightsaber clashes. This sec-tion looks at ways to increase the drama of a discussion, negotiation, or similar encounter.

The drama of a situation is naturally increased when both sides have something important to lose or gain by the outcome. Striking a balance between something that is important enough to add drama, but not quite enough to start a fight over, can be challenging. What is important to one character in one situation may not be important to another character or even the same character in a different situation.

Prior to the scene, the GM should determine what the PCs involved might find important. It could be an item, a person, a vehicle, a culture, or an ideal. Once selected, the GM then works out how the NPC might view the same thing. Even if the NPC isn't particularly interested in the selected subject, he might become interested to challenge, thwart, or simply irritate the PCs.

Once the scene begins, the GM should encourage a serious tone to the conversation and actions. Humor isn't banned, and in fact can add to the drama and tension when used well (see **Using Humor in Social Encounters** on the next page). However, the NPCs should return to a serious tone after any attempts at humor. The more critical or important the situation, the more serious the NPCs should act, and the more responsive they should be.

During the scene, the NPC's emotions should usually be apparent. Unless the characters happen to already be established as unemotional, they should show their feelings on their sleeves to help communicate their responses. Emotional characters are generally more interesting and give the PCs more opportunities to react and interact appropriately.

Drama is derived from conflict. When setting up a social encounter, the GM should keep in mind that most involve some sort of underlying conflict. It might be as minor as drawing information out of a reluctant informant, but sometimes, the two parties are bitter enemies with little reason to trust each other, let alone talk something out. GMs should determine the underlying reasons why there is conflict in a given scene or discussion, and use that undercurrent to help drive NPC motivations and reactions to PC negotiating tactics and attitudes.

USING HUMOR IN SOCIAL ENCOUNTERS

Humor is among *Star Wars'* greatest traits. When used effectively, it adds great entertainment value at the gaming table. A lot of humor occurs naturally, with players and characters exchanging quips or barbs at each other's expense, or at the situation in general. Interaction between the GM and the players can have equally amusing moments as their characters antagonize each other and build on each others' comments.

Creating a scene with a mix of humor and drama requires careful pacing. This can be hard to achieve when the GM doesn't control every character in the encounter, unlike a movie scene or written story. However, it is possible to plan some shifts between drama and humor through pre-generated read aloud text, or for the GM to trigger certain events or comments based on predetermined actions and expected discussion points. Two common scenarios are:

- Build tension, build tension, build tension, introduce unexpected humor, then suddenly increase tension!

- Build tension, build tension, then break tension (with humor).

The GM should also determine when not to intentionally use humor. While he cannot keep the PCs from interjecting their idea of fun into an encounter, dramatic moments are usually best used without laugh out loud humor. Some villains in the *Star Wars* movies share in the occasional amusing moment at their own expense, but most major villains do not—especially those using the dark side of the Force. Darth Vader never laughs. When the Emperor laughs, it is strictly at his own cleverness and superiority, never at himself or at his own expense. Everyone else should be terrified at the thing he finds so amusing.

Creating situations for humor to blossom is very challenging, as comedians or amusing storytellers can attest. Below are a few suggestions that might help.

Some extend beyond the social encounter and into encounter design in general.

Droids: Droids are traditional and natural sources of humor in *Star Wars*. Droids are created and programmed to succeed at specific tasks. Any situation in which they are attempting a task they are ill suited or not programmed for means they are likely to struggle and make mistakes. Droids with unexpected cleverness, such as R2-D2, also ramp up the humor as they turn their limitations into unexpected assets. Malfunctioning droids also add to the humor, as they do unexpected things or expected actions very poorly. Some examples of droids providing humor are presented here:

- Malfunctioning translator—perhaps the droid speaks every few words in an obscure, unknown language, suddenly forgets a language, uses the wrong dialect, or gets stuck on an unbearable accent—or even switches between accents.

- Personalities—Droids with over the top personalities or personalities counter to their function, size, or abilities are often amusing. Examples include arrogant protocol droids, medical droids afraid to conduct surgery, and overly aggressive mouse droids. Such personalities can go too far, so the GM should be ready to rein them if it begins to wear on players' nerves.

Malfunctions and other disruptions: A sudden mechanical malfunction at just the wrong moment can interject humor into many social encounters. While these can cause a variety of emotions and conditions, malfunctions that turn a bad situation into something impossibly worse are often good fun. Cascading malfunctions—where one thing after another goes bad in some related fashion—can ratchet up the humor and drama of a situation at the same time. Continually failing lights or power, quirky computers, and glitchy holographic projectors are easy targets for creating small moments of amusement and frustration.

Humorous species: Though bumbling Gungans are not the norm for their species, any species' physical or cultural quirks can become the source of humor when combined with the need for negotiation and discussion. Imagine an enormous Gamorrean, famous for their dim-wittedness, trying to navigate the oddities of buying items from a quick witted Toydarian with questionable goods. Jawas provide humor through their deeds (taking apart whatever they can get their hands on at any moment) and their negotiations (when their trade goods suddenly fail or fall apart at just the wrong moment). This pits extreme differences of personality, cunning, culture, size, and more against each other.

COLONIST CONTRACTS

Unlike other careers, which have criminal or military backgrounds, Colonists contextualize their world through civilian and corporate culture. As such, their work is usually outlined in a written or verbal contract. Colonists prefer contracts that create recurring payments and repeat business, but such work is rare and the bidding for them is fierce. Most Colonists are forced to take side jobs performing a wide variety of tasks to stay solvent.

This section presents potential contracts and jobs for Colonists. A contract usually covers the time period of an entire adventure, though multiple smaller jobs might take place within larger adventures. While these contracts are designed for Colonists, other characters may take supporting roles or participate as equals, depending on their backgrounds and goals.

PICKING AT SCABS

The PCs are hired by a Chevin mining tycoon to mediate a settlement with his disgruntled employees. The miners went on strike, and when the Chevin replaced them with independent labor, the miners turned violent and barricaded themselves inside the mine. The miners are threatening to collapse the mine if their demands aren't met. The PCs must enter the mine and hear the workers out to reach a settlement.

Part 1: The PCs are visiting or operating in the area when they are contacted by a desperate wife of the mine foreman. She has taken up a collection from all the miners' families, and hopes the PCs can talk sense into her spouse and the owner. While she knows it isn't much, she suggests the Chevin owner should at least match her offer. Once the PCs finalize their contract with the Chevin as independent mediators, they can go to the mine.

Part 2: The mine shaft is bored directly into the side of a mountain. Next to the mountain is an abandoned staging area littered with heavy machinery and even a couple bodies of miners and strikebreakers. Evidence of a bloody, close-fought battle is all over the site; blood-soaked picks, shovels, and drills lay next to the corpses. The main entrance is guarded by a pair of miners sporting blaster rifles, and the turbolift is disabled at the bottom of the shaft. The PCs must convince the guards to call the lift, then meet with the leader of the strike-turned-lock-in, and hear his demands. The miners are demanding better pay, fewer hours, better job security, better working conditions, better protective gear, and pardons for the accidental death of any of the scab workers who tried to take over the work site. They also oppose the use of slave labor, which is where the Chevin got his replacement workforce.

Part 3: The PCs must return to the Chevin with the list of demands and negotiate on the miners' behalf. The Chevin is shrewd and stingy, and sees no reason he shouldn't stick with his slave labor. After convincing the Chevin to make some concessions, the PCs must take the counter-offer back to the miners. If all their demands are met, only a Simple Negotiation check is required. For each demand not met, increase the difficulty of the check one step. If the negotiations fail, the miners resolve to take down the Chevin by force, and if that fails, destroy the mine. The PCs must choose whether to help the miners, the Chevin, or bow out and let the two sides destroy each other.

Twist: The mine itself is rich with a unique material used exclusively by an organization the party opposes, perhaps a metal unique to the Empire like an element of quadanium steel, or an explosive used by the Rebellion such as baradium. This means that at least one person in the party should want to see the mine collapsed or otherwise shut down.

SPLITTING HEIRS

The Party is hired to locate a missing teenaged heir to House Demici on Serenno. The boy's recently widowed father suspects his rivals, House Nalju, though he tends to suspect them of everything. During their investigation in Nalju territory, the party is captured and accused of espionage, but learn House Nalju is not responsible for the boy's disappearance. A raid by Noble Guards wearing House Demici colors ends with the abduction of the heir to House Nalju, leaving the PCs to figure out what is going on and put a stop to it.

Part 1: The PCs are contacted by the leader of House Demici to locate his missing son and only heir. After negotiating their compensation, the PCs can search the boy's chambers and talk to his educators, chefs, and servants to gain perspective on the missing boy and his possible whereabouts. The party learns he set out to hunt split-tail dorsalope with a dozen of his Noble Guard. The path leads toward House Nalju territory, which confirms Count Demici's suspicions.

Part 2: While following the trail, the party is captured and brought to a House Nalju encampment. The camp is led by the teenaged heir of Count Nalju. He claims to be investigating a sighting of House Demici Noble Guard, but has yet to find anything. Young Nalju says he would gladly escort the young lord home if he found him, in order to avoid war between their houses. Depending on the actions of the party, Nalju tells the PCs they are to be taken to his father for questioning or escorted back to Demici territory in the morning. Either way, in the middle of the night, the camp is attacked by House Demici Noble Guardsmen. In the ensuing battle, the party witnesses the heir to House Nalju being stunned and dragged off into the forest.

Part 3: The PCs must sneak after the kidnappers. They can follow the trail several days on foot to a canyon. Inside, guards from both houses are working together. The party can surrender, fight, or sneak past the guards. Once inside, they discover the two heirs have allied to drive their houses to war. They plan to kill their fathers during the confusion and take over their respective houses. After a brief arms race, the two young heirs could unite their houses and dominate Serenno.

The PCs can try to convince the boys to surrender, fight them to a standoff, or simply escape to get word to their fathers. However, convincing the Counts of their sons' treachery should prove difficult without indisputable evidence.

Twist: Count Demici is in possession of an item or ability to help alleviate the Obligation of a party member.

POLITICAL PARTY

The PCs are hired by a senior political aide named Vil Kargaims to perform at a Fete Week celebration. The event doubles as a re-election campaign for the leader of a small colony world, and as such includes dozens of campaign staff and supporters during the planning. There is an unnamed air of tension to the preparations that comes to a head when Vil Kargaims is murdered. Everyone on the property is a potential suspect except the PCs. The sheriff and governor lock down the mansion and ask the party to lead the investigation.

Part 1: The PCs are contacted by the campaign manager Vil Kargaims to put on a performance during a re-election campaign rally at the governor's mansion during Fete Week. After negotiating a fee and any other concessions, the PCs are given early access to the grounds to rehearse. At the mansion, the party meets several influential members of the colony, including the Governor, his top aides, the sheriff, rancher barons, and other influential locals. They also meet a supporter the campaign staffers call "Big Bantha," thanks to his massive campaign donations in past elections. He is a die-hard fan of any Performers in the party, and Kargaims hopes to impress him enough that he donates big credits this year. The performance can be heard throughout the building, but is interrupted by sounds of blaster fire. Moments later, the party learns that Vil Kargaims was just murdered.

Part 2: The mansion is immediately locked down by private security under direction of the sheriff. Unfortunately, the sheriff can't account for her whereabouts during the murder, claiming she was in the refresher. Since everyone was able to hear the rehearsal at the time of the murder, only the PCs are above suspicion. With the sheriff recused from the investigation because she is a potential suspect, the governor deputizes the party to carry out the investigation. Questioning all the potential witnesses eventually leads the party to discover the following information:

- The governor had an affair with a junior aide, which Kargaims discovered.

- Kargaims was a notoriously bad sabacc player, and owed credits all over town, including a large sum to a rancher.

- When not on the campaign, Kargaims was a barrister, and recently condemned a woman to death over a speeder crash fatality. The woman's husband is on the catering staff.

- "Big Bantha" is a friend and supporter of the governor, but a deeper look reveals that many of the policies the governor is currently pushing jeopardize "Big Bantha's" stranglehold over the local markets. Chief among these plans is a trade agreement with a neighboring system.

Part 3: The PCs must go over their evidence and decide who is responsible for Kargaims' murder. The conclusion the PCs are most encouraged to reach is to blame the condemned woman's husband, who then claims the governor put him up to it to cover up his affair. The truth is that "Big Bantha" conspired to have the husband take the fall so the governor will lose the election. His opponent is against the trade agreement. "Big Bantha" promised the husband that the new governor would pardon him and his wife. The PCs must decide how much discretion to exercise, as evidence of the affair has a good chance of dashing the governor's re-election hopes as completely as allegations of a murder conspiracy.

Twist: A party member owes obligation or has some sort of background tie to "Big Bantha." He uses leverage on the party member to make sure the bereaved husband and the governor's affair with his intern are both discovered and tied to the slain campaign manager as motives.

FRONTIER CLAIM

One of the PCs is granted a parcel of land for a reason that makes sense within the context of the campaign. The land includes a cave system supposedly rich with minerals and gems, though its location carries some inherent dangers. Unfortunately, upon arrival, the party discovers the land and the buildings on it have been overrun by a squatting swoop gang.

Part 1: The PCs receive a message about their inheritance. Upon their arrival at the inherited parcel of land, the party finds well over two dozen swoop bikers and a dozen hangers-on scattered across the property. They have broken in and ransacked the buildings, and have been squatting there for weeks, turning the rustic homestead into something closely resembling the scene of a high-speed podracing crash. Upon discovery of the party, the gang members turn hostile, but the PCs can try to bluff, bully, or negotiate their way to an audience with their leader. The party should try to convince the bikers to move on, but they seem itching for a fight. Fortunately, the gang seems unaware of the potential fortune in gems and minerals within the caves.

Part 2: Depending on how the PCs dealt with the gang, they either have control of the homestead or are forced to sneak past the bikers to the caves. Either way, exploration of the cave system is dangerous; Scholars and Doctors should recognize some hazards, including deadly spores, sinkholes, and insect life. Navigation of the cave system is likewise complicated, requiring spelunking equipment or repulsorpack assistance. Despite the dangers, if the PCs press on, they should be allowed to discover a lode of rich minerals or gemstones they can sample to have tested in town a few hundred kilometers away.

Part 3: Upon exiting the caves, the PCs run into the swoop gang, this time with a more aggressive leader. The swoop gang followed the PCs after their previous encounter. If the party destroyed the gang with no survivors, then it is instead a rival gang. The bikers seem intent on eliminating the party and claiming the gems for themselves, and are unlikely to allow much negotiation. The gems are quite valuable, worth tens of thousands of credits (or able to pay off 5-10 Obligation).

Twist: The swoop gang leader is somehow related to the character who inherited the homestead, or at least to the person who bequeathed it. He would seem to have a legitimate, almost equal claim to the property.

COLONIST CAMPAIGNS

This section contains ideas and advice for conducting socially focused campaigns for Colonists. Unlike campaigns centered on other careers, Colonist campaigns favor social challenges over the heavy use of combat or other skill types. These campaigns might depend on the party to direct a colonization effort, help a struggling colony, or follow the story of a particular group of settlers. PCs can even build their own homestead from scratch, then watch it grow in size and complexity until its influence rivals that of any land baron in the sector.

COLONIST BASE OF OPERATIONS RULES

A key component to early colonization efforts of any planet is the homestead; it is an independent colony in miniature, operated by a hardy group of individuals living communally. Homesteads are often owned and operated by large families or clans, though it is not uncommon for homesteaders to hire on additional hands, particularly for harvest and auction seasons.

Despite countless variations to account for functional environmental needs and individual aesthetics, most homesteads have a similar design. There is always a main house around which the rest of the homestead is arranged, known as the main campus. The main house functions as home to either owners or the entire clan. This is often the largest building on the main campus, and doubles as an administrative and meeting space.

Homesteads also have several support buildings near the main campus. These often include dormito-ries, workshops, power generators, water treatment facilities, and a chow hall that is part cafeteria and part lounge. As the homesteads grow, children and favored hands are often granted small parcels of land to tend as their own. These families may even purchase the land outright, forming homesteads of their own. Eventually, this may create a true community.

The second key component to successful colonies is a business. Once several homesteads have grown large or close enough to form a community, businesses crop up to meet their needs. These businesses tend to be small and self-sufficient; with the first tending to a broad spectrum of customer needs (general stores) and later businesses focusing on a particular area of commerce.

CREATING A HOMESTEAD OR BUSINESS

In Colonist campaigns, there is a good chance that the majority of the campaign takes place on a single planet, limiting the utility of a party starship. In lieu of a ship, players may wish to establish a business in town, or to create their own homestead. These locations can be used as a headquarters for the party, fulfilling a similar role to the party starship. If the party begins play with a homestead or business instead of a party starship, all costs are waived.

First, the party should determine whether their base of operations is a homestead or a business. Once the party has selected a headquarters type, the next step is to determine the focus. For homesteads, the party must choose an animal to ranch, a crop to farm, or a resource to mine (this might even be something like asteroid mining with a private space station). Busi-

DARKLIGHTER ESTATE

Huff Darklighter, father of rebel hero Biggs Darklighter, manages the most powerful homestead on Tatooine, the Darklighter Estate. Sprawling across over a thousand square kilometers and located just southwest of Anchorhead, the homestead primarily deals in hydroponic farming. The estate also includes dozens of moisture farms run by sharecroppers, which allows the Darklighters to acquire water for their hydroponic farms at cost. Huff is always looking to expand his operations, and currently has his eyes on the Lars Homestead, which borders his territory.

One of the biggest advantages the Darklighter Estate holds over other homesteads on Tatooine is its ownership of a weather satellite dedicated to monitoring its region. This orbital assistant allows Huff to detect incoming sandstorms

and even nomadic bands of Tusken Raiders and Jawas long before they arrive. That no disaster has arrived unannounced has been the difference between zero losses and financial ruin more than once for the Darklighters.

Like many homesteads on Tatooine, most of the Darklighter Estate is underground, with a large, open-air courtyard. There are upwards of four dozen hands and family members on the estate at any given time, and including sharecroppers, Huff has well over one hundred able-bodied beings under his care. The Darklighter patriarch takes pride in his reputation for throwing lavish feasts, where all his hands leave full and contented. It is a saying amongst moisture farmers that on Tatooine, only Jabba's rancor eats better than those on the Darklighter Estate.

BASE OF OPERATIONS OBLIGATION

The Obligation earned when improving a base of operations is group Obligation, which means it is Obligation belonging to all the Player Characters in the party. This means that when this Obligation triggers, each PC suffers the effects of his Obligation triggering.

Generally, when the base of operations Obligation triggers, the narrative events should relate to the base of operations. This could be as simple as unexpected bills or an afternoon of repairing moisture vaporators on the South Ridge. Alternatively, it could involve a rampaging gundark breaking into the pastureland or a rival mining baron deciding to execute a hostile takeover of the PCs' land. The GM is free to make the narrative effects of the Obligation triggering minimally invasive, if it would distract from an important ongoing plotline, or an unexpected and major issue for the PCs to deal with immediately and personally.

One possibility the GM can keep in mind is that a prominent upgrade for a base of operations is profits for the PCs. If the base of operation's Obligations triggers (and particularly if it rolls doubles), the GM might decrease the amount of money the PCs make off their base of operations that month due to the unexpected costs or slumping profits.

nesses instead select an entertainment venue, a retail store, or a service shop. In both cases, the chosen focus determines a specific skill that becomes a career skill for all party members (representing their familiarity with the type of work the homestead focuses on). The party can then spend credits or undertake additional group Obligation to improve their base of operations. The various abilities can provide a steady stream of credits for players, or make new resources or services available to the party between adventures.

The headquarters can be more than just a mechanical benefit to the party. Many improvements add an NPC to the base of operations that the party can get to know between adventures. These NPCs can then be used to help kickstart new adventures and encounters. Perhaps the children of the homestead's mining foreman have gone missing, and the PCs must form a search party to locate them. A regular customer at the party's cantina was mugged after leaving the previous evening, and it is up to the party to investigate and make sure their patrons are safe. A customer brings in a blasted-up droid into the party's droid shop, but during repairs, the party discovers the details of a plan to begin spice refining and distribution near town.

THE COLONIST BASE OF OPERATIONS

When the base of operations is first purchased, the party gains the basic base of operations. The base of operations also has a series of upgrades the party can purchase for additional credits or Obligation. Each additional Obligation increases the magnitude of the original Obligation taken to pay for the base of operations, instead of becoming a "new" Obligation.

The upgrades are presented on **Table 3–4: Homestead Upgrades** and **Table 3–5: Business Upgrades**. Each upgrade has a description of the upgrade, and a cost in credits or Obligation (the players select how they would like to pay for the upgrade when they select it). These upgrades may be purchased in any order at the beginning of any session, as long as the GM says the purchase makes narrative sense (purchasing a new garage while the party is in the midst of a protracted combat with bandits wouldn't make sense, for example, since the garage may take a week or two of uninterrupted work to build). If it makes sense that the upgrade would take time to install, or involve adding a new NPC to the base of operation, the GM handles this narratively.

HOMESTEAD

To start a homestead, the party chooses the location where they would like the build the homestead and a core function they would like to serve: ranching, farming, mining, or something similar. Ranches focus on raising animals for pets, food, or labor. Farms grow crops for food or industrial purposes. Mines extract natural resources from the environment. The particular animal, crop, or resource can be determined by the players and the GM. The party might have a nerf ranch on Delaya, a hydroponic farm on Tatooine, or a tibanna gas mine on Bespin. It is also possible to use the homestead rules to represent a small commercial space station run by the party. In this case, the station usually sells consumables, repairs, and entertainment to passing ships (although this could also be considered a business, its self-sufficiency makes the homestead rules more appropriate).

Basic Homestead: The basic homestead includes a main house, kitchen, power generator, water well, and a living quarters. It also attracts one NPC employee per party member, and includes an area up to ten square kilometers that is suitable for the selected focus of the homestead. In the case of a space station, it includes a hangar bay as well as quarters for the crew, and instead of ten square kilometers, it has accommodations for ten visitors and two docking tubes that can connect to visiting spacecraft.

Basic Homestead Cost: 50,000 credits and 5 Obligation. These costs are waived if the homestead is selected in lieu of a ship at character creation.

TABLE 3-4: HOMESTEAD UPGRADES

Upgrade Type	Upgrade Description	Upgrade Cost
Increase Core Focus	The size and scope of the homestead grows, increasing the scale of operations and the profits for those invested in it. If the homestead is a ranch or farm, the land area may increase, mines may dig additional tunnels, and a space station may expand in size. Alternatively, the homestead may hire more employees or invest in better technology and infrastructure. Once a month, each PC in the party receives 100 credits in profits from the homestead. This upgrade may be taken up to four additional times, each time increasing the profits received by 100 credits.	2,500 credits or +2 Obligation
Improve Security	The homestead's security improves, better protecting the people within. When this upgrade is purchased, select one of the following: • All buildings (or doors within the space station) gain electronic locks that can only be broken with a **Hard (♦♦♦) Computers check**. • The homestead gains a security droid (See **Edge of the Empire** Core Rulebook page 412). • The homestead gains reinforced fences around the main buildings, or if it is a space station, it gains shields granting it defense 1. • The homestead gains security cameras that can be accessed from a central control room. This upgrade may be purchased two additional times, each time selecting a different option.	10,000 credits or +2 Obligation
NPC Ally	The homestead includes an NPC ally who can help the party with certain tasks. This may be an employee of the party, or a wandering merchant or doctor who decides to settle at the homestead for a time. When this upgrade is selected, choose one of the following: • A NPC merchant who can obtain items (some of dubious legal value) for the party. The merchant has a Presence of 3, Cunning of 3, 2 ranks in Negotiation, and 2 ranks in Streetwise. He can obtain and sell any legal or Restricted item with a modified rarity of 5 or lower to the party. • An NPC doctor who can heal characters on the homestead and treat ailments. The doctor has an Intellect of 3 and 2 ranks in Medicine. He has medical supplies allowing him to perform Medicine checks without penalty. • An NPC mechanic who can repair items, droids, and starships and vehicles. The mechanic has an Intellect of 3, 2 ranks in Mechanics, and 2 ranks in Computers. He has a tool kit allowing him to perform Mechanics checks without penalty. • An NPC pilot who can pilot ground or space vehicles for the party. The pilot has an Agility of 3, an Intellect of 2 and 2 ranks in Piloting (Planetary), 2 ranks in Piloting (Space), and 2 ranks in Astrogation. If the GM needs a full profile for these NPCs, he should assume they have a 2 in all other characteristics, 1 rank in the party career skill determined by the homestead (unless it would be higher due to their selected profile), and no ranks in any additional skills. This upgrade may be taken three additional times, with a different NPC being chosen each time.	2,000 credits or +1 Obligation
Infirmary	The homestead includes an infirmary, stocked to handle any major accidents or outbreaks of disease. The infirmary includes beds for several patients, medical supplies (allowing characters to perform Medicine checks without penalty), and a bacta tank with a supply of bacta. This upgrade can only be taken once.	5,000 credits or +3 Obligation
Mechanic's Garage	The homestead includes a garage where mechanics can make repairs on vehicles and droids. The garage includes a full set of mechanic's tools (allowing characters to perform Mechanics checks to heal droids or repair starships without penalty), and an oil bath for droids. When used to repair starships or vehicles, the character repairs 2 additional hull trauma or 2 additional system strain on a successful check. This upgrade can only be taken once.	5,000 credits or +3 Obligation
Landing Bay	The homestead includes a landing bay able to hold starships or vehicles. This may be an open landing bay, an enclosed hanger, or a pressured docking bay with a mag-con field for a space station. The landing bay holds a number of vehicles with a combined silhouette of 15, with no single vehicle larger than silhouette 5. This upgrade may be taken up to two additional times. If taken additional times, this can either represent additional landing bays, or increase the combined silhouette limit of the original bay by 15 (although the maximum vehicle size remains at silhouette 5).	3,000 credits or +1 Obligation

Party Career Skill: The party must select one homestead focus. The focus determines the career skill granted to the entire party: Farm (Resilience), Ranch (Survival), Mine (Athletics), Space Station (Piloting [Space]). Each character in the party counts this skill as a career skill.

BUSINESS

Not all campaigns work thematically with the isolated and insular nature of a homestead. An alternative is to open a business in town, where the party can regroup between adventures and be a part of a larger community. To create a business, the party chooses both a location and a focus for it. The different business focuses are entertainment, retail, and service. Entertainment venues include cantinas, nightclubs, casinos, and restaurants. Retail shops stock and sell a single category of gear, such as ranged weapons, melee weapons, armor, communications, detection devices, medical, cybernetics, recreational entertainment, security, survival, tools, droids, ground vehicles, airspeeders, or starships. Service businesses might include a repair shop, medical clinic, gym, adventure travel firm, consulting firm, a taxi stand, or countless others.

Basic Business: The basic business includes a main floor for customers, a back room for storage, and either an upstairs or basement the party can use as a living area. It contains the basic equipment needed to operate the business (a medical clinic might include cots and basic medical supplies, a repair shop may include lifts and repair tools, and a retail shop would include shelves and basic retail stock). It also includes one employee or droid per party member.

Basic Business Cost: 50,000 credits and 5 Obligation. The costs are waived if selected in lieu of a ship at party creation.

Party Career Skill: The party must select one business focus. The focus determines the career skill granted to the entire party: Entertainment (Charm), Retail (Negotiation), Service (choose either Mechanics, Computers, or a single applicable Knowledge skill for the entire party). Each character in the party counts this skill as a career skill.

TABLE 3-5: BUSINESS UPGRADES

Upgrade Type	Upgrade Description	Upgrade Cost
Increase Core Focus	The size and scope of the business grows, increasing the scale of operations and the profits for those invested in it. The size of the building may increase, the business may hire more employees, or it may make investments in infrastructure and technology. Once per month, each PC in the party receives 200 credits in profits from the business. This upgrade may be taken up to four additional times, each time increasing the profits received by 200 credits.	2,500 credits or +2 Obligation
Improve Security	The business's security improves, better protecting the people within. When this upgrade is purchased, select one of the following: • The business's doors, windows, and outbuildings gain electronic locks that can only be broken with an **Hard (◆◆◆) Computers check**. • The business gains a security droid (See **Edge of the Empire** Core Rulebook page 412). • The business's main buildings are constructed of heavily reinforced materials, giving it an armor value of 2 (weapons unable to do more than 2 planetary scale damage cannot damage the buildings). • The business gains security cameras that can be accessed from a central control room. This upgrade may be purchased three additional times, each time selecting a different option.	10,000 credits or +2 Obligation
Special Orders	The business increases its ability to obtain hard to find items relating to the business's focus. When attempting to find an item that relates to the business (how this applies exactly is up to the GM), the item's rarity decreases by 2 (in addition to other modifiers). This upgrade can only be purchased once.	2,000 credits or +1 Obligation
Wholesale Prices	The business gains the ability to purchase items in bulk with a discount. When purchasing bulk orders of legal items that have a modified rarity of 4 or lower, the total price decreases by 10 percent. The amount constituting a "bulk order" is up to the GM, but should be at least 10 large items such as speeder bikes or portable entertainment systems, or 100 small items such as pre-packaged meals or comlinks. This upgrade can only be purchased once.	1,000 credits or +1 Obligation
Specialized License	The business gains a specialized license, allowing it to conduct activity that may normally be restricted, licensed, or illegal. The nature of this license depends on the business and the world the business is located on (as not all worlds find the same activities illegal), but it could include selling Restricted items, weapons, or armor, running a casino, or operating a private security force or mercenary outfit.	2,500 credits or +2 Obligation

COLONIST CAMPAIGN IDEAS

The following sections contain campaign ideas that GMs may adapt and expand upon for their own games. Each section addresses a different take on Colonists, their group size, and their specializations. While the main players are described, the GM must create their stats or use similar stats from the **Edge of the Empire** Core Rulebook. This allows the GM to fully customize the scenario to the difficulty level appropriate for the PCs, whether they are starting new or are heavily experienced.

NEUTRAL PRACTICES

The PCs are hired by the Refugee Relief Movement to reopen a hospital within an active war zone between local factions. The hospital has been looted, but survived air strikes intact. The RRM hopes to provide care for civilians, particularly those caught in the crossfire, and intends to produce a public relations campaign around the wounded to assist in fundraising across the galaxy. The PCs must come up with creative solutions for dealing with the supply shortages, attempts to commandeer the hospital, and any unexpected repercussions their actions might create.

Possible Location: The suggested location is a small city in the Rim at war with the Empire, or any location with victims of natural disaster or internal strife. Some suggestions would include cities on Begeren, Jabiim, Ord Biniir, Sullust, or any world within Bothan Space.

Employer: Refugee Relief Movement, an organization formed three decades prior that once helped to relocate and care for the victims of natural disasters and those caught in the middle of the Clone Wars. The RRM still operates in much the same way, but goes to great lengths to make certain they are not seen as Rebel sympathizers through a policy of strict neutrality.

Enemy Forces: The enemy forces are mostly looters, disgruntled patients, and both warring factions, be it the Empire and Rebellion or two local factions.

Starting amount for payment negotiation: The RRM realizes the inherent danger of this effort, and there are very few beings with the desired skills willing to go. The price starts at 20,000 per PC upon completion of the contract, though PCs can negotiate for up to 25,000, with 5,000 up front, or for some additional supplies. The RRM also provides food and supplies for the three month job.

Campaign Objectives: The primary objective is to get the city hospital back to operational status, and to provide civilians with shelter from the fighting. The hospital needs an emergency room, a clean room for surgery, a long term care ward, a cafeteria, and a refugee shelter. Each of these locations requires power and staffing. The RRM has also given strict instructions to keep the hospital neutral, fearful the Empire might label them rebellious.

Episode I: An RRM missionary contacts the PCs and offers them the job. Their first task is to shuttle to the planet and establish an operations center at the hospital. The RRM has secured an Imperial escort from the landing site to the hospital, and players can meet the Imperial Commander (or Imperial-allied side) and learn about the conflict.

Upon arriving at the hospital, the PCs need to clear out any squatters and get the supplies inside and secured before they are raided. Members of the party should be designated various positions, including the Director of Hospital Services (potentially for Politicos), Chief of Medicine (a good position for Doctors), Chief of Medical Research (a potential Scholar position), Chief of Security (possibly for Marshals), Chief of Logistics (potentially for Entrepreneurs), and Chief of Public Outreach (a reasonable position for Performers). Each of these department heads can also have assistants, with medical professionals being the most valued commodity. The party also has to set up an emergency room and put out feelers to recruit personnel with medical training to assist. Note that the party only has the labor and resources to set up one ward per episode.

Episode II: The next job is for the party to spread the word that the hospital re-opened under the neutral protection of the RRM. The Chief of Medical Research discovers that the limb-loss injuries are the biggest single issue. These patients require more than just emergency care, meaning a long term care ward is a priority. Alternatively, the party can repair the rooftop shuttle landing pad, saving a trip to the edge of town for resupply, though stores are currently full. Amidst this effort, an Imperial officer enters the hospital with a squad of walking-wounded troopers shuffling behind him. If his men are given immediate treatment, the Commander promises to get some medical supplies diverted to the PCs. This would clearly violate the RRM's neutrality rule, but would provide much needed help to wounded civilians.

Episode III: The PCs next need to help staff the hospital with medical personnel, as word is spreading and the work load is getting too large for the party to handle the patients alone. If the PCs helped the Imperials in the last episode, they could contact the officer and ask if any Imperial surgeons and medics might volunteer to pull some shifts. Otherwise, the Chief of Public Relations can speak with the mayor about any doctors, surgeons, nurses, or medical droids that might still be in the area. A trek through the city, with some luck and good investigation, can yield a number of medical droids (including the mayor's own), a former military doctor in the planetary militia, and a cosmetic surgeon. The party must also choose between setting up a clean room for surgery, which would increase survivability and reduce the rate of infection during surgeries, or shelter for displaced civilians, which could prevent future injuries and deaths, but put undue strain on food and water supplies.

Episode IV: Supplies have begun to run low, and unless the party has repaired the landing pad, the PCs must meet the supply ship several kilometers outside of the city. Also, a wounded Imperial agent named Galway stumbles into the supply exchange. Agent Galway claims he is not with the military, and is investigating rumors of slave traders taking advantage of displaced civilians. While talking with Galway, a band of brigands that allegedly wounded him attack the supply exchange or hospital proper. There are many patients whose lives depend on the supplies getting back to the hospital, and the PCs should prioritize protecting the crates.

Also, the party must choose between putting resources into building a cafeteria or a communications array. The cafeteria can improve morale and feed refugees. Alternatively, the long-range communications array can send images and data back to the RRM to begin their PR campaign, which makes additional supplies available in the next episode.

Episode V: With the fighting over, the Imperial agent asks the party to be his temporary deputies to help him track down and put a stop to the slaving activity. He accompanies the party as they talk to half a dozen or more locals who tell stories of others being abducted and never seen again. Eventually they track the slavers to their lair, and the party realizes, after watching for a moment, that it is actually a Rebel recruiting and resistance operation, not a slaver operation. The missing people were new recruits being sent offworld. The party must decide what to do with this information, and whom to side with. The party can also select any hospital improvement they passed on in a previous episode to add this time. After returning to the hospital, the RRM delegate that hired the party arrives with the next crew, evaluates the PCs'

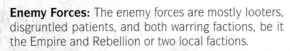

performance, and gives them the remainder of their payment, if any.

IMPERIAL AGENT GALWAY

Agent Galway is an Imperial special agent in charge of rooting out illegal enslavement of sentient beings according to Imperial law. More often than not, Agent Galway finds himself protecting enslaved humans. He is young, idealistic, and believes all of mankind should be free. Of course, he hasn't given much thought to the slavery of non-humans. However, he is a hero to many freed former slaves on the fringes of Imperial Space, and both a gifted investigator and combatant. Agent Galway is not ready to consider the hypocrisy of Imperial-sponsored enslavement of the Mon Calamari, Wookiees, and others, and confronting him on this issue pushes him to anger.

IMPROVING STATION

The PCs travel to Gandanta Station, an obscure shadowport and home to thousands, to meet with a Toydarian fence to sell a recently acquired item. Unfortunately, the PCs' ship is stolen almost immediately, leaving them stranded. The PCs are forced to do odd jobs for the Toydarian until they get back on their feet. The work presents opportunities for the PCs to make contacts within Black Sun, which eventually co-opts the party into taking over the station in its name. Of course, being a Black Sun asset comes with its own problems. The PCs must decide if they want to stay with Black Sun, ally with the Hutt Cartels, go independent, or turn legit.

Possible Location: Any large space station can work, but the Phaseera System in the Lantillian Sector provides an ideal location.

Employer: Flummot, a Toydarian

fence. Later (in Episode II), the PCs may be employed by a Black Sun underboss.

Enemy Forces: Only the ones the party makes along the way.

Starting amount for payment negotiation: 100 credits per party member, negotiable up to 150, though each job is worth progressively more.

Campaign Objectives: Turn disaster into destiny and grow a dying shadowport into a thriving center of trade, illicit or otherwise.

Episode I: The PCs arrive on Gandanta Station to meet with a Toydarian fence named Flummot, only to discover their planet of origin recently reported an outbreak of Sangi Fever. The quarantine protocols require immediate isolation and testing of the PCs and a decontamination sweep of their ship. However, when the PCs return from medical, they find the ship has been stolen. Flummot arrives in the docking bay, takes pity on the PCs, and offers them a job. Flummot needs some stolen artwork validated before he buys it, as well as some extra muscle for the transaction. The PCs negotiate the terms of the job, and Flummot gives them a general rundown of the station and a brief tour. The deal is with some Black Sun agents, who allegedly "acquired" the artwork from the Tion Hegemony.

Moments after the PCs verify the authenticity of the art, a gang of Hutt thugs interrupt the meeting, and Flummot is wounded. The PCs must get Flummot and the paintings to safety, while the Black Sun agents engage the bulk of the enemy.

Episode II: Impressed with the PCs' skills and grateful for saving his life, Flummot offers to introduce the PCs to the Black Sun underboss—a Trandoshan named Raken—assigned to oversee Gandanta Station operations. He wants the party to work with Black Sun to oppose Hutt Cartel rule over the station. Their first mission is to discover the identity of their ambushers and their source of information. The PCs have to skulk through multiple cantinas and Hutt fronts without

revealing their true motives to avoid a cantina brawl. Eventually, the PCs discover that there is a homing beacon in Flummot's chance cube.

Episode III: The underboss wants to use the chance cube as a trap. He has the PCs spread word that Flummot is making a paradigm-shifting deal later that night. That evening, the PCs don breathers and mag boots and carry the chance cube from Flummot's to a small hangar bay where they hide. When Hutt forces storm the hangar, a Black Sun agent is supposed to slice the hangar door, sucking the enemy out into the void. However, as the hangar fills with enemies, it becomes clear that something has gone wrong on the Black Sun agent's end. One of the PCs must get to the controls and slice the door.

Episode IV: With the Hutt's security detail in shambles, the underboss offers to install the PCs as the new leaders of Gandanta to run day-to-day operations for Black Sun. This first requires going directly to the Hutt in his throne room and convincing him to leave the station. The Hutt is obstinate, but without many thugs left, he can be intimidated. The PCs can also be reminded that the Hutt was in charge when their ship was stolen or impounded, and this is a chance for them to reclaim their ship and its contents. With the

Hutt ousted, the party now runs the station for Black Sun, and has a small contingent of Black Sun thugs to help keep order.

Episode V: Black Sun has begun using Gandanta as a major interchange for moving arms and spice. They have also strong-armed some local systems to use the station for their legit shipment needs, to provide more cover for the increased activity. Additionally, the Hutt Cartels have sent a young upstart to negotiate rights to use the station for some of their smuggling efforts. Finally, Black Sun agents report that a pair of Sector Rangers have recently come onboard and begun nosing about the station in response to the increased activity. The PCs must find a way to get rid of both the Hutt presence and the Sector Rangers, preferably by setting them against each other.

Episode VI: It has become clear to the PCs that they are an expendable resource to Black Sun, and they should break ties with the vast organization. Any attempt the party might make to board their ship is met with resistance from Black Sun agents, and they find that they are as much prisoners as rulers on Gandanta. The party can hatch their own escape plan, or, if they want to maintain control of the station, they have a few other options. They can contact the Sector Rangers and exchange their testimony in exchange for pardons and a life in witness protection. They can turn to the Hutt Cartels, who would favor neutral leadership of Gandanta over Black Sun cronies, though that would likely incur additional Obligation. They can also try to hire mercenaries or recruit an army of local thugs and scum to oppose the Black Sun presence and take over the station for themselves.

UNDERBOSS RAKEN

While it is unclear just which Vigo Black Sun underboss Raken works for, no one questions his affiliation or his prowess. A hulking Trandoshan, Raken has a calm, quiet menace that sets him apart from most of his species. He is brilliant, cunning, and ruthless in the execution of his master's orders, and completely amoral. He is also a vicious combatant, and has been trained by some of the best unarmed combat instructors and marksmen credits can buy.

GOING NATIVE

The PCs are sent to study a recently discovered aboriginal species to determine if they deserve full rights as sentient beings by the Imperial Xenodetic Survey Department. While primitive, the natives understand some aspects of sentient life, and the PCs find themselves relating to the primitives more than the colonists that discovered them. However, the colony has a vested interest in the natives being classified as semi-sentient so they can exploit rich aurodium deposits on native land. As the PCs grow closer to the indigenes, the mayor moves toward a violent resolution to the dispute, with the PCs caught in the middle.

Possible Location: Any planet that is host to both colonists and a primitive or semi-sentient species works, but planets like Dandelo, Dantooine, Gigor, Maridun, Malastare, Nelvaan, or Sluudren are all fine examples.

Employer: Imperial Xenodetic Survey Department (Formerly the Republic Bureau of Xenology)

Enemy Forces: Colonists and local wildlife.

Starting amount for payment negotiation: 3,000 credits per PC, negotiable up to 4,000 credits per PC.

Campaign Objectives: To determine the level of sentience of the native species the colonists have discovered, and determine their ability to incorporate into galactic society.

Episode I: An Imperial Xenodetic Survey Department (XSD) spokesman contacts the PCs and offers them the job. Once the PCs negotiate terms, they are shuttled to the settlement that discovered the new species. Governor Danisher greets the party and discusses what he knows of the natives, why they weren't spotted during initial surveys, and their current location. The PCs have time to tour the settlement, gather supplies, and hire a guide to escort them to native territory.

Episode II: The party is guided through the brush and learns about the local flora and fauna, which might provide insight into the native culture and lifestyle. The guide's way of teaching the PCs to survive should contrast later with the aboriginal way. The guide has a low opinion of the indigenes as ruthless savages, citing many stories and a few personal encounters. After a few days' ride, the PCs clear a hill overlooking the native village. If the PCs lack a protocol droid, the guide speaks some basic words in their language, but his limited vocabulary adds ■ to any social skill checks he translates. The PCs must convince the warriors that ride out to challenge them that they are peaceful, and should meet with their leader. If successful, the guide departs, and the PCs are brought to the tribal leader, who has an aide that speaks broken Basic. The PCs must convince the chieftain and his advisors that the party is not a threat, and to get permission to stay and observe them in their daily lives.

Episode III: The PCs spend a week observing the natives, recording notes, and conducting some sentience tests provided by the XSD. By this time, all party members can make an **Average (♦ ♦) Knowledge (Education) check** or an **Easy (♦) Knowledge (Xenology) check** to see if they have learned the native tongue. Those that have not, suffer ■ to ■ ■ ■ when making any social skill checks without a dedi-

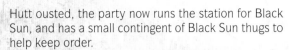

cated translator, but are still capable of basic conversation. The party is invited to join some natives on a hunt. The creature can be giant and fierce, stealthy and cunning, or just skittish game, but the hunt proves difficult for the party. PCs successful in the hunt feel a stronger connection to the people and their way of life afterward.

Episode IV: The party bids the tribe farewell and returns to the colony to report their findings. Over a formal dinner, Governor Danisher asks the PCs about their experience. He then reveals he has recently discovered rich deposits of aurodium on native land. He intends to strip-mine the region, and the PCs must convince him to negotiate a settlement first. Meanwhile, Danisher tries to convince the party to classify the natives as semi-sentient. Appealing to his better nature is unlikely to have any impact, but playing to his greed or personal interests can be effective.

Episode V: Depending on the outcome of the last episode, Governor Danisher and his army of colonists are either racing the party back to the village or camped a few kilometers away, awaiting the party. When the party returns to the natives' village, whose scouts have already seen the colonist army, they are looked upon as traitors. The PCs must convince the chieftain and his advisors that it is in their best interests to either flee or to work out some kind of deal with the mayor to let him mine the aurodium. The chieftain sees wisdom in this, but his council of elders believes it can defeat the colonists. It is up to the PCs to avoid a war that is likely to wipe out the natives.

GOVERNOR FILLEN DANISHER

A ruthless veteran of previous corporate colonial efforts, Fillen Danisher was given his Imperial governorship thanks to the patronage of Grand Admiral Grant. Danisher served under the Grand Admiral as his liaison to the Imperial Army before a brief stint as a project lead for the Imperial Mining Corporation. There he led coordinated efforts to strip-mine resource rich worlds across the galaxy. He is cunning, intelligent, unflinching, and doesn't think twice about killing innocents to achieve his goals.

HOW THE REST WAS WON

The PCs are hired by the Imperial Colonization Board (ICB) to evaluate a failing colony and get it back on track. Colonists have reported the land isn't arable, people are starving and succumbing to illness, and without anything to trade, merchant traffic has yet to arrive. The PCs are given a month to turn the struggling settlement around, otherwise the ICB must evacuate the colony.

Possible Location: Any newly established colony world in Wild Space or the Unknown Regions works.

Employer: Imperial Colonization Board.

Enemy Forces: Local wildlife.

Starting amount for payment negotiation: 5,000 credits per PC, negotiable up to 6,000 credits per PC.

Campaign Objectives: Place the colony back on the road to survival and growth.

Episode I: An Imperial Colonization Board (ICB) representative contacts the PCs and offers them the job. Once the players negotiate terms, they are placed on a shuttle bound for the ailing colony. The party arrives to empty streets and silent storefronts. The colony doctor died of renal failure, and most colonists are suffering from disease brought on by starvation. The PCs come across a boy named Jek who is in better shape than most, and he explains that the crops never took root, and then the plague hit. The PCs have been given a fresh batch of supplies by the ICB, which makes addressing the plague the top concern. If the party has a Doctor or Scholar, this is the moment for them to take center stage with a series of checks that require a gathering of samples from settlers and local wildlife to synthesize a serum or vaccine.

Episode II: Within a week, most of the colonists have regained their strength, and are pleading with the party to call in an evacuation ship to take them back home. It is up to the PCs to inspire the frontiersmen to conquer their fear and solve the food shortage together. This again requires the PCs to gather samples of the seeds that wouldn't take root, but even with the help of all the settlers, no seeds can be found. It turns out there is a colony of ant-like insects that have been stealing and eating the seeds. The PCs can come up with a geographical, chemical, or physical solution, or perhaps an animal tested in Episode I is effective at rooting out and eating the ants. Regardless of the method, a week after the solution is found, the new crop begins sprouting.

Episode III: With the settlement approaching sustainability, the colonists have begun to have hope for the future again. Still, without a steady flow of merchant traffic, the colony has little hope for long-term survival. The PCs must identify what resources the world has that are unique to the sector, and help the Colonists set up the enterprise. If successful, the party can contact the ICB to spread word about the commodities available for trade at the colony. The PCs' mission is considered a success when the first merchants land.

COLONIST JOBS

Many Colonists have some experience holding down a full time job, and in some games, they may still have the opportunity to work while participating in adventures. Most Colonist jobs are salaried or contracted in advance, providing the Colonist more job security than most. The more remote the colony, the more an employer prefers to pay partially in goods or services, but the contract's value should remain competitive.

When negotiating a labor contract, use **Table 3–6: Colonist Pay Scale**, which presents a broad range of jobs undertaken by Colonists and their range of pay. GMs should feel free to adjust costs as needed, taking into consideration variables like environmental hazards, employee reliability, and the employer's resources. Remember, these are simply guidelines to help GMs set reasonable pay rates. Also keep in mind that even though these are themed towards Colonists, any PC can take on one of these jobs if the ongoing narrative allows for it.

Some of these jobs have a pay rate based on completion of the job, while others have a monthly or daily pay rate. In both cases, the GM should keep in mind that the PC needs to spend a significant amount of time working to earn this money. If the pay rate is a monthly salary, the PC should have been working most of the month to make the salary. If the pay rate is based on performing a specific task (negotiating a contract or performing a surgical operation), the PC must complete that task to certain agreed upon specifications.

Of course, full time work does not make a very interesting game. Therefore, if the PCs decide they want to hold down full time jobs, the GM can take one of the following approaches. He can determine that the PCs work at their full time job during campaign "down-time," and have the actual game sessions represent a few days out of every month. In this case, the PCs can be assumed to be working a regular job in the interim.

On the other hand, the GM can weave the PCs' jobs into the ongoing narrative. This may not work for some jobs, however other jobs lend themselves to entertaining and interesting plots. For example, if the PCs are working as the mayor, sheriff, and doctor of a small town, they could have plenty of adventures just keeping the small town prosperous and safe; fighting off bandit attacks, surviving dangerous storms, negotiating with the local Imperial garrison, and driving off local predators. Plenty of police procedurals, doctor dramas, and other episodic television shows use the formula of the characters being confronted with extraordinary circumstances in their everyday jobs.

OTHER REWARDS

During the course of a job, Colonists may be loaned tools and equipment. In most cases, these materials belong to the employer, and are to be returned upon project completion. However, should the Colonist break borrowed equipment, the cost is typically deducted from his salary over several installments. Most freelancers are expected to supply their own tools, and ill-preparedness on the part of a Colonist is often reflected in his pay.

Expensive equipment the Colonist can't realistically pay for can be handled via additional Obligation. The Marshal serving as town sheriff is given access to a jail, armory, and speeder pool. While these resources are his to deploy at his discretion, he is obligated to use them to protect the town. The Dutybound or Responsibility Obligations in an amount consistent with the resources granted work well in these instances. The same could be said of a Politico moving into the Mayor's estate, the Scholar taking over the town library, or the Doctor put in charge of the town hospital and its assets.

Many colonies are poor in credits, but rich in other resources, particularly land. New colonies may try to

---

CORE WORLDS, THE OUTER RIM, AND COST OF LIVING

The pay rates set in **Table 3–6** are kept broad and simple for ease of use. However, some groups may want to modify those pay rates based on other factors. For example, jobs on the Core Worlds tend to pay more, but jobs on the Outer Rim planets tend to offer more autonomy. Another issue PCs and the GM should consider is cost of living. Realistically, some of the money PCs earn in their jobs has to go towards food, shelter, and other expenses.

If the GM wants to account for location when determining pay rates, he should increase the pay rate for jobs on a Core World by 20 percent and can decrease the pay rate for jobs on an Outer Rim (or other uncivilized planet) by 20 percent.

If the GM wants to account for living expenses, he can also deduct 25 percent of the PCs' pay rate to go toward food, living quarters, and so forth. This is easier than trying to track individual expenses, although if the PC in question is living particularly frugally or extravagantly, the GM can adjust this percentage as he sees fit.

TABLE 3-6: COLONIST PAY SCALE

Job	Job Description	Duration	Pay in Credits
Small Town Sheriff	A lawman who protects a small town with a handful of deputies.	Monthly salary	2,000-3,000
Police Commissioner	A lawman who protects a small city, with dozens to hundreds of men working underneath him.	Monthly salary	3,000-5,000
Deputy	A low-ranking deputy in either a small town or a larger city.	Monthly salary	750-1,200
Detective	A detective serving in a public constabulary or police department.	Monthly salary	2,000-2,500
Private Eye	A private investigator working on a single case, generally a non-criminal situation. Private investigators are often hired to investigate marital infidelity, corporate espionage, or potential political scandals.	Daily salary	75-200
Mechanic	A mechanic working in a small repair business for vehicles and items.	Monthly salary	1,000-2,000
Town Doctor	A doctor providing treatment of injuries or illness to a small town.	House call	100-300
Licensed Physician	Working in a hospital or other professional treatment facility. Typically characters must have at least 3 ranks in Medicine to earn this salary.	Monthly salary	2,000-4,000
Surgery Team	Performing a single complicated surgery at a hospital, such as a cybernetic replacement or operation to repair major trauma. Typically the group must have at least 4 ranks in Medicine amongst them to earn this salary.	Single operation, group rate	5,000 (not including materials)
Single Performance	Live entertainment for a single evening by jugglers, acrobats, artists, musicians, puppeteers, actors, or comedians.	Single event, group rate	500-750
Cantina Band	Live mood music for a cantina or restaurant, with a long term contract.	Weekly salary, group rate	1,000-1,500
Touring Band or Entertainment	Live original music for an evening performed by a touring band. Pay is based almost entirely on fame and demand, but skill is also a factor. (This category can also be used for other types of high profile performance.) Typically, the group must have at least 5 ranks in Charm and/or Cool amongst them to earn this salary.	Single event, group rate	2,000-25,000
Street Performer	Tips earned by jugglers, acrobats, artists, musicians, puppeteers, actors, or comedians.	One day's worth of tips	25-75
Lecturer	Teaching students a particular topic in an institute of higher learning.	Monthly salary	1,500-3,000
Subject-Matter Expert	Working as an expert witness, consultant, data compiler, or other subject-matter expert on a per-job basis. Typically, characters must have 3 ranks in a specified Knowledge skill to serve as a subject-matter expert.	Single Job	750-5,000
Researcher	Researching a specific topic or developing a new design or item. Research could range from pure knowledge at a university to developing a new product in a corporate lab. Typically, characters must have 3 ranks in a specified Knowledge skill to serve as a researcher.	Monthly salary	2,000-8,000
Mediator	Mediating disputes and legally arbitrating disagreements between two individuals or corporations. Such arbitration can take days, or even weeks, and must be accepted by both parties. Typically, characters must have 2 ranks in Negotiation to work as a mediator.	Single dispute	2,000-5,000
Negotiation Team	Mediating major disagreements or even hostilities between large corporations or even governments. Such arbitration can take weeks or even months, and must be accepted by both parties. Typically, the group must have 3 ranks in Negotiation amongst them to earn this salary.	Single dispute	4,000-20,000
Mayor or Councilor	The political leader of a small town or community. The mayor can be expected to handle any number of administrative tasks.	Monthly salary	2,000-3,000
Clerk	An office laborer or retail clerk.	Monthly salary	1,000-1,500
Miner	Experienced mining laborer.	Monthly salary	1,000-2,000
Ranch Hand	A ranch hand skilled in herding or shepherding livestock. Typically, characters must have 2 ranks in Survival to serve as a ranch hand.	Monthly salary	1,500-2,000
Unskilled Labor	Basic manual labor.	Monthly salary	500-750

bargain land in lieu of payment in hard currency. The land costs the colony nothing to give, so the work is obtained essentially for free. Further, owning the land often convinces the professional or business to stay to develop the property. This improves the colony's local economy and skilled-labor resources, all at no cost.

Colonies are also fond of trading goods. To those just passing through, colonies offer alternative payment in a locally sourced commodity. Many independent merchants make planetfall carrying repulsor and droid parts, datapads, medicine, and holovids, then leave with a hold full of ore, textiles, foodstuffs, and native artwork, which they can sell for a healthy profit elsewhere.

When dealing with each other, Colonists often trade services, sometimes on credit. Helping a rancher falsely accused of murder win his case might not pay any credits, but his lawyer can expect to feast for free on the largest shaak the rancher has during Fete Week, or at the very least find his house has a freshly painted fence. In this way, a Colonist might accumulate and trade favors and services that integrate him tightly into the community, proving the wealth of a colony is in its populace, not its vaults.

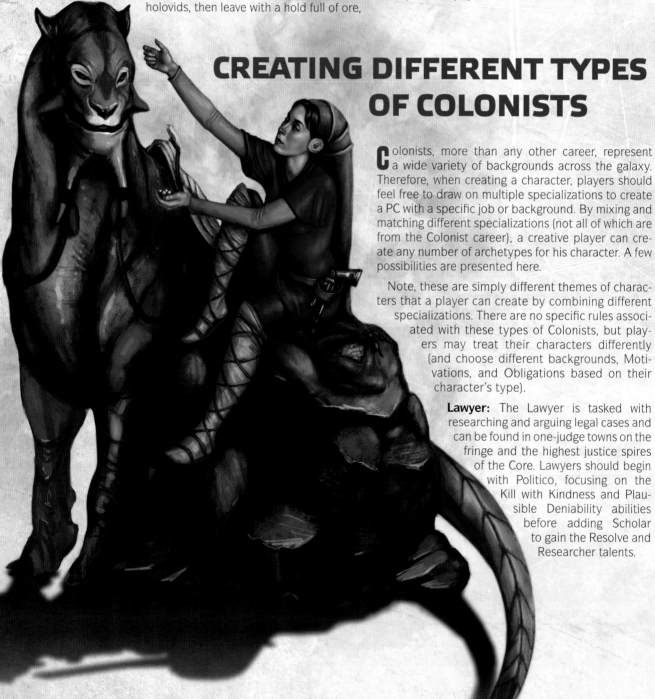

CREATING DIFFERENT TYPES OF COLONISTS

Colonists, more than any other career, represent a wide variety of backgrounds across the galaxy. Therefore, when creating a character, players should feel free to draw on multiple specializations to create a PC with a specific job or background. By mixing and matching different specializations (not all of which are from the Colonist career), a creative player can create any number of archetypes for his character. A few possibilities are presented here.

Note, these are simply different themes of characters that a player can create by combining different specializations. There are no specific rules associated with these types of Colonists, but players may treat their characters differently (and choose different backgrounds, Motivations, and Obligations based on their character's type).

Lawyer: The Lawyer is tasked with researching and arguing legal cases and can be found in one-judge towns on the fringe and the highest justice spires of the Core. Lawyers should begin with Politico, focusing on the Kill with Kindness and Plausible Deniability abilities before adding Scholar to gain the Resolve and Researcher talents.

Chop Doc: Some doctors specialize in surgically installing and repairing cybernetic limbs. Chop Docs should begin with Doctor, focusing on the Master Doctor and Natural Doctor abilities before adding Outlaw Tech to gain the Tinkerer and Inventor talents.

Engineer: Engineers create new technologies and improve on existing ones, but do most of their work on a datapad rather than in a workshop. Engineers should begin with Scholar, focusing on the Knowledge Specialization, Respected Scholar, and Researcher abilities before adding Outlaw Tech to gain Tinkerer and Inventor talents.

Field Scientist: Not all science can be done in the lab, and many scientists operate in the wild, where they test real-world results instead of laboratory ideals or datawork hypotheticals. Field Scientists should begin with Scholar, focusing on the Researcher, Knowledge Specialization, and Brace abilities before adding Survivalist to gain the Forager, Expert Tracker, and Outdoorsman talents.

Private Investigator: Private Investigators are dedicated to using their unique talents to solve crimes and support the rule of law. Private Investigators should begin with Marshal, focusing on the Bad Cop, Street Smarts, and Unrelenting Skeptic abilities before adding Thief to gain the Bypass Security and Stalker talents.

Intelligence Agent: Information obtained through stealth and subterfuge is the province of the Intelligence Agent. Intelligence Agents should begin with Scholar, focusing on the Brace and Well Rounded abilities before adding Thief to gain the Bypass Security, Indistinguishable, and Master of Shadows talents.

Intelligence Analyst: Corporate and military analysts comb through data to recognize trends and predict future outcomes in markets and military actions alike. Intelligence Analysts should begin with Scholar, focusing on the Natural Scholar and Researcher abilities before adding Slicer to gain the Bypass Security, Codebreaker, and Technical Aptitude talents.

Laboratory Researcher: Chemists, physicists, biologists, and metallurgists all spend countless hours researching and testing in their labs, making breakthroughs that might shower them with credits or places in history. Laboratory Researchers should begin with Scholar, focusing on the Knowledge Specialization, Respected Scholar, and Researcher abilities before adding Slicer to gain the Technical Aptitude and Natural Programmer talents.

Magician: Misdirection, sleight of hand, and showmanship are what make for a legendary stage magician. Magicians should begin with Performer, focusing on the Smooth Talker and Natural Athlete abilities before adding Scoundrel to gain the Hidden Storage, Natural Charmer, and Convincing Demeanor talents.

Sheriff: Sheriffs exercise their authority to deputize others to keep the small towns of the frontier safe. Sheriffs should begin with Marshal, focusing on the Good Cop, Quick Draw, and Unrelenting Skeptic abilities before adding Mercenary Soldier to gain the Command and Field Commander talents.

Sector Ranger: Avatars of justice with almost limitless jurisdiction, the Sector Ranger can track lawbreakers from the Core to Wild Space and beyond. Rangers should begin with Marshal, focusing on the Street Smarts, Good Cop, and Quick Draw abilities before adding Scout to gain the Disorient, Shortcut, and Quick Strike talents.

Tribal Chieftain: Before urban civilizations rise, and after they fall, sentients usually exist in tribal communities. These groups demand a combination of intelligence and strength from their leadership. Tribal Chieftains should begin with Politico, focusing on the Kill with Kindness, Inspiring Rhetoric, and Improved Inspiring Rhetoric abilities before adding Mercenary Soldier to gain the Command and Field Commander talents.

JOIN THE REBELLION TODAY!

STAR WARS
AGE OF REBELLION
ROLEPLAYING GAME